Editor
Mary Kaye Taggart

Editor Project Manager
Karen J. Goldfluss, M.S. Ed

Editor-in-Chief
Sharon Coan, M.S. Ed

Illustrator
Karon Walstad

Art Direction
Elayne Roberts

Cover Artist
KeithVasconcelles

Project Manager
Phil Garcia

Imaging
Pete Sadony

Publisher
Mary D. Smith, M.S. Ed.

5/21 W9-DJP-628

Rain Forest

EXTENDED THEMATIC UNIT

Authors:

Ilene Miller and Laurie Agopian

Teacher Created Resources, Inc.
6421 Industry Way
Westminster, CA 92683
www.teachercreated.com
©1995 Teacher Created Resources, Inc.
Reprinted, 2006
Made in U.S.A.
ISBN-1-55734-674-7

Table of Contents

Introduction

Welcome to the world of the tropical rain forest, teeming with rare species of animals and plants that exist nowhere else on earth. Located between the Tropics of Cancer and Capricorn, rain forests are characterized by hot, humid weather all year long, which creates an environment conducive to an abundance of growth. Typically, the yearly rainfall is more than eighty inches, with some areas reaching more than two hundred inches in one year. Temperatures hover between 70° and 85° Fahrenheit (21° and 29° Celsius).

Hundreds of years ago, tropical rain forests encircled the globe, much like long green arms, hugging the equator and covering twenty percent of the earth's land surface. Reduced to a mere six percent, the diminishing rain forest shelters more than one half of all of the plant and animal species living in the world today. Rapid deforestation has endangered the splendor of this tropical paradise.

A rich diversity of life abounds in the tropical rain forest community. By comparison, the rain forest supports more species per acre than any other habitat found throughout the world. Still thriving in the rain forest are the vibrant colors and exotic sounds of many plants and animals that have disappeared from other parts of the world.

In this study of the rain forest, students will learn about the interdependence of the plant and animal life that is so unique to this environment. Today's changing world has created new challenges for the survival of the rain forests.

Overview of the Unit

Rain Forest is an in-depth, integrated (multi-disciplinary) thematic study of life in the rain forests around the world. This exciting unit contains a wide variety of teaching suggestions and reproducible pages which are adaptable to any level—elementary through high school.

This thematic unit includes activities in social studies (map skills, geography, environmental issues, etc.), science, math, language arts (including poetry, creative writing, letter writing skills, etc.), creative arts, and cooking. These activities encourage cooperative learning. The first page of sections two through eight contains introductory information, extension ideas, and a table of contents for the section.

Suggestions and patterns for transforming the classroom into a tropical rain forest and setting up a "Rain Forest Museum" are included. This will enable students to synthesize their knowledge and share it with an entire school population and the community.

The unit allows students the opportunity to experience all modes of communication: reading, writing, listening, observing, illustrating, and public speaking. Through this integrated approach, students will learn and retain more as they practice and apply their skills in meaningful contexts.

Introduction *(cont.)*

What Is Thematic Teaching?

The first step in thematic teaching is choosing a theme. This theme will be your focus in developing a unit of study to incorporate multiple curriculum areas. Learning experiences should relate to each other and to the needs of the classroom.

The central theme should have a broad area of focus. It should be adaptable to as many areas of study, concepts, and skills as possible. A good theme will not only allow flexibility in planning, but will also help students to understand the connection between the subject areas.

Thematic teaching allows all learning experiences to be interrelated and more meaningful to the student. The content of thematic units can be abstract or concrete, complex or simple. The unit is organized in such a way that a wide variety of curriculum areas are integrated into a coherent whole. Incorporated into this process are higher-level thinking skills, open-ended activities, hands-on projects, cooperative group interaction, writing, research, and individualized learning.

Why an Extended Unit?

Themes can last one day or an entire school year. *The Rain Forest* is a year-long, multi-disciplinary, multiple intelligence unit of study. Many of the sections included in this book can be used as independent mini units.

Rain Forest allows for in-depth study. Since the theme is ongoing, children are given an opportunity to become extremely knowledgeable about the topic. A wide variety of activities are available to meet each student's needs. Additional resources are provided that will allow you to enrich your program.

Thematic teaching allows the learning environment to be one that promotes independence, autonomy, and student focus. When students work cooperatively on related but different activities, as offered in this book, there is less negative competition and the classroom environment is more productive and harmonious.

Rain Forest provides an opportunity to study a theme that, throughout the school year, will allow integrated learning and will relate to the real needs and experiences of the student. It also provides community and global awareness and involvement.

Meet the Rain Forest

This section focuses on the locations of the tropical rain forests and their characteristics.

Why Are Our Rain Forests So Special?

- The rain forests cover only six percent of the earth's land surface, yet they are home to more than half of the plant and animal species on earth. Many of those plants and animals are waiting to be discovered. Too many are becoming extinct.

- Almost half of all medicines which are used today originally came from the rain forests.

- The rain forests are a major source of wood for the world.

- The rain forests provide many food products.

- The vegetation of a rain forest is so diverse that you can walk for over a mile without ever encountering the same species of tree twice.

- Nearly two hundred million people around the world derive their livelihood from hunting and gathering in the rain forests or from cultivation within and around their fringes.

Suggestions for Extending the Section

- Give the students a list of animals and have them research the layer in which each animal lives. Make this activity a contest by giving a prize to the group who finds the most animals.

- Have students write individuals or agencies, requesting information about some aspect of the rain forest. (See resources on page 167.)

Contents of This Section

Tropical Rain Forests of the World, Where Are You?

Rain forests are found in a band twenty degrees north and south of the equator. This area is called the tropics because it is always hot and wet.

Look at the map (page 169) and answer the following questions.

1. The equator is found between the Tropic of _____ and the Tropic of_____ .

2. Are the rain forests of Central America found north or south of the equator?

   _____

3. Are the rain forests in South America found north or south of the equator?

   _____

4. Which ocean would you cross to travel from Africa to South America?

   _____

5. Which three continents do not have tropical rain forests?

   _____

6. Does Australia have a large rain forest as compared to South America?

   _____

7. Which continent is west of the Indian Ocean?

   _____

8. True/False: Europe has two rain forests.

   _____

9. True/False: Rain Forests are located on some islands in the Pacific Ocean.

   _____

10. True/False: Rain Forests are located near the equator.

   _____

Layers of the Rain Forest

The rain forest is made up of a complex system of layers which includes trees, shrubs, vines, ferns, and other plants. There is no distinct boundary between the four layers which include *forest floor, understory, canopy, and emergent layer.*

Forest Floor:

The forest floor is carpeted with a soft layer of moss, decaying leaves, and fallen branches. The air in this layer is very still as there is no wind. The thick forest canopy, towering 65 feet (20 meters) above, keeps the forest floor dark even in the daytime. The humidity on the forest floor is always above 70%, making it very muggy here. The average rainfall in tropical rain forests is over 80 inches annually, and the temperature remains constant between 70° to 85° Fahrenheit (21° to 29° Celsius).

The soil in the rain forest is not very fertile. The constant heavy rainfall washes nutrients away quickly before they can be absorbed into the ground. Therefore, root systems are very shallow so they can quickly recycle nutrients.

Ferns, mosses, gingers, and other plants that need very little sunlight grow on the forest floor. Only two percent of the sun's rays filter down to this level. The forest floor is surprisingly free of green vegetation due to the lack of sunlight. Lianas (woody vines) that wind around the forest trees root here.

The animals on this level survive on decomposing dead materials that have fallen from the other levels. There are lots of insects here: beetles, ants, termites, centipedes, millipedes, and spiders, to name a few. Also found on the forest floor are: worms, rodents, larger mammals, frogs, toads, poisonous snakes (such as the fer-de-lance), armadillos, and caimans (a reptile that looks like an alligator).

Layers of the Rain Forest *(cont.)*

Understory:

Ten to twenty feet (three to six meters) above the forest floor is the understory layer of the rain forest. It is almost as dark here as it is on the forest floor. The humidity is still high here in the understory and the temperature remains constant.

Small trees and shrubs abound in the understory. The trees at this level have elongated crowns like the flame on a candle. The leaves on the trees are large, enabling them to absorb the diffused sunlight. Some trees will remain at this level their whole lives. Others wait for an opening in the canopy layer created by fallen trees. This opening provides the sunlight and space necessary for the trees to grow to the upper levels.

Fruits and nuts are found growing at this level, which attracts many animals. The animals found here cling, leap, swing, and fly from branch to branch. Spider monkeys and tamanduas (anteaters) hang by their tails in this layer. Many animals have adapted to living in the understory. For example, the red-eyed tree frog has special pads on its toes to enable it to cling to trees, flying squirrels have flaps of skin between their toes that help them glide from tree to tree, and anole lizards have long toes with sticky pads which make them good climbers.

Larger mammals (such as jaguars and ocelots) also live at this level where they can find a plentiful supply of small animals for their diet. Many snakes, such as the tree boa and the false coral snake, make their homes here in the understory where they do their hunting at night (which means they are nocturnal). Most insects live here in the understory, becoming part of the food chain for such predators as iguanas, other lizards, snakes, etc.

This abundant supply of insects also feeds the tropical bat population. Each bat can eat up to three thousand insects per night. Other bats drink nectar from flowers growing here. As the bats drink the nectar in the flowers, they pick up pollen. When they land on their next flower, some of the pollen falls off, thus pollinating the flowers. Still other bats eat tropical fruits. They germinate the rain forest because they eat and eliminate seeds as they fly.

Canopy:

Sixty-five to one hundred feet (20 to 30 meters) high above the forest floor is the canopy with its flat-topped trees. Here neither the temperature nor the humidity stays at a constant level. The canopy forms a continuous green covering over the rain forest with its twisting and turning leaves. It acts like a giant umbrella filtering out all but two to five percent of the sunlight and rain.

Layers of the Rain Forest *(cont.)*

The tall trees growing in the canopy layer are supported by a special root system. Some of these trees have round stilt roots while others have buttress roots. The leaves on the trees up here become very wet. Therefore, they have developed special drip tips that allow the water to run off. This keeps their surfaces dry so that molds, lichens, and small plants will not grow on them.

The canopy layer is full of incredibly beautiful plants and flowers like orchids and bromeliads. The bromeliad leaves grow out of its center, forming a bowl. This bowl collects rainwater, thus providing nourishment and a home for salamanders, frogs, birds, and insects.

The canopy layer is like a giant wildlife park. Most of the plants and animals of the rain forest can be found here. There are spider monkeys, sloths, opossums, loud howler monkeys, colorful butterflies, moths and thousands of birds, including parrots, hummingbirds, paradise tanagers, big billed toucans, screeching macaws, and oropendolas. Many birds make nests in the hollow trunks of trees to hide from predators. These animals call the canopy home.

Emergent:

Towering above the canopy, anywhere between 115 to 150 feet (35 to 46 meters) high, is the emergent layer. One acre of rain forest contains only one or two of these giant trees. Some of these trees can grow up to 250 feet (76 meters) high, like the tualang (TOO-ah-long) of Malaysia. The trees are supported by tall, slender trunks and either thick-ridged buttress roots or circular stilt roots. These trees sport umbrella-shaped crowns.

High above the canopy these towering giants of the rain forest must deal with low humidity, strong winds, and high, changing temperatures. There is constant exposure to the sun's rays. The small, thick, and waxy leaves of these trees are able to retain water in this harsh environment. The small leaves are aerodynamically designed to allow air to move around them.

These skyscrapers of the forest are home to the harpy eagle and morpho butterfly. The few fruits and flowers that are found here take advantage of the winds for pollination and dispersal of their seeds.

Layers of the Rain Forest *(cont.)*

Activity

Create a three-dimensional display showing the four layers of the rain forest: the forest floor, the understory, the canopy, and the emergent layer.

Directions:

1. Color the pictures. Cut along the bold outlines.

2. Fold on the dotted lines so that the pictures can stand up.

3. Glue the colored pictures, below the dotted line, onto a piece of 6 inch by 9 inch (15 cm x 23 cm) tagboard. Place them one behind the other in the following order: forest floor, understory, canopy, and emergent layer.

Layers of the Rain Forest *(cont.)*

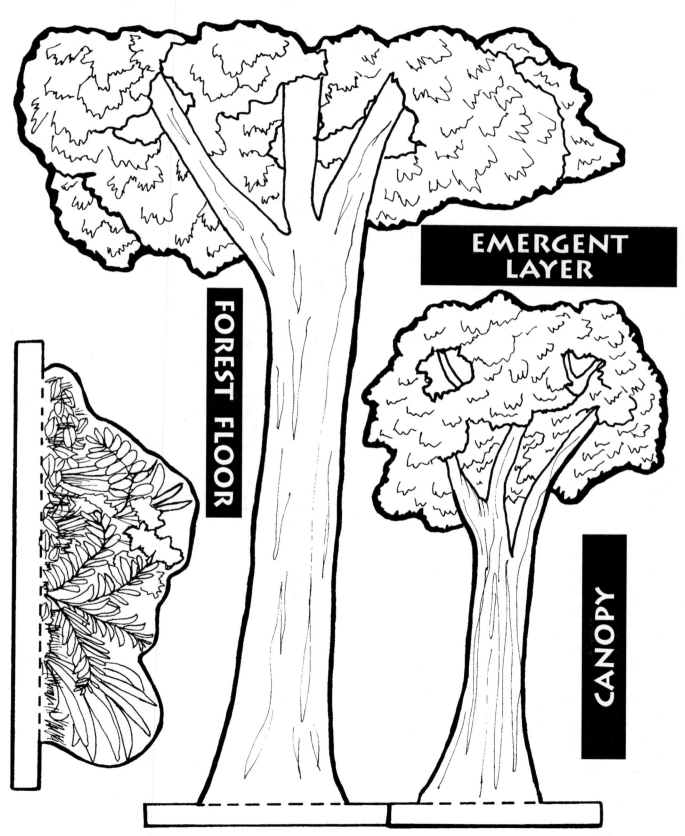

EMERGENT LAYER

FOREST FLOOR

CANOPY

Just My Size

Visualizing the enormous size of many rain forest trees is sometimes difficult to do. For example, the African mahogany tree is 200 feet (61 meters) tall and the koompassia of Southeast Asia can grow to 272 feet (83 meters) tall. The koompassia is the tallest rain forest tree.

Activity

1. Predict how many students would be needed to reach the height of a chosen giant rain forest tree if each student stood on the other's head.

2. Using a partner and a measuring stick, determine your height.

3. Collect the heights of all the students in your class and find the average height.

4. Using this new information, once again predict how many students would be needed and compare this to the original prediction.

Activity

1. Using either a meter stick or a yard stick (or both for comparison), measure and mark with chalk the correct height of a giant rain forest tree onto the school grounds.

2. Draw a rain forest tree to size using this measurement.

Challenge:

- Based on the height of the tree, convert yards to feet and inches. Convert meters to centimeters. Compare these.

Activity

1. Students may form a line along this drawing by lying head to foot for the entire length of the tree.

   - How many students did it actually take to reach the length of the tree?

   - How does this number compare with your other predictions?

2. Display your prediction and final outcome on a graph.

3. A photograph can be taken of the chalk tree and line of students. An interesting angle would be from the roof of the school.

Challenge:

- Even though the African mahogany and the koompassia trees are the largest in the rain forest, the largest tree in the world is the sequoia. Extend your graph to include the sequoia tree (which can reach 400 feet or 122 meters). Compare the information about the sequoia trees to that of the rain forest trees.

Jungle Journeys

Jungle Junket

Take a geographical research trip into a rain forest country.

1. Select a country which has tropical rain forests.

2. Research the country to find the following information:
    - ❖ population
    - ❖ climate
    - ❖ economy
    - ❖ major exports
    - ❖ culture
    - ❖ food

3. Suggested resources: public library, embassies, airlines, travel agents, and ethnic restaurants.

4. Present the research using one of the following forms: poster, diorama, shoe box movie, skit, puppet play, etc.

Tropical Trivia Trek

- Make up 12 Tropical Trivia questions about the tropical rain forest.

- In teams of four, put questions together and play a question and answer quiz game. As a variation, give the answer first and have the contestant give the question in return.

The Lorax

- View the video *The Lorax* by Dr. Seuss and discuss the message behind the story.

You Can't Grow Home Again

- View the Emmy award-winning video of the Costa Rican rain forest, *You Can't Grow Home Again* by 3-2-1-Contact (Children's Television Workshop). Discuss what can be done to help the rain forests survive. To order the one-hour VCR tape, write to: The Video Project, 5332 College Avenue, Suite 101, Oakland, CA, 94618, or phone (415) 655-9050.

Rain Forest Rap

- View the six-minute video rap called *Vanishing Rain Forests*. To order, write to: World Wildlife Fund, P.O. Box 4866, Hampden Post Office, Baltimore, MD, 21211, or phone (301) 338-6951.

Lost in the Wild

Teacher Note: This guided visualization would be enhanced by the use of a tape of soft rain forest sounds and a darkened room. Have your students find a comfortable position. Guide them in taking slow, deep breaths to relax. When you are ready, read the following narrative to the class.

Guided Visualization

You are about to embark on an imaginary journey through a tropical rain forest. As you travel, try to visualize the sights, sounds, and smells of the jungle. Since there are many mysterious surprises in the jungle, make sure you bring your safari hat, binoculars and, of course, your machete (a very sharp knife).

As you approach the jungle, you see a thick wall of greenery. Using your machete, cut a path into the foliage to make an entrance. It is an emerald green world in here, so very dark and beautiful. Look up and see the green roof of the canopy layer high above. The air feels heavy and wet, yet cool. Listen! What do you hear? The sounds of birds screeching, monkeys chattering, and a million buzzing insects. What a symphony of sounds!

The sound of running water in the distance lets you know that there is a waterfall nearby. Suddenly, you are startled by the crashing sound of a branch falling through the trees.

Walking along the forest floor feels like walking on top of wet, squishy sponges. There are damp moss, the odor of decaying leaves, and branches crunching under our feet. Be careful; it can be very slippery here on the forest floor. Even though it is the middle of the day, it is dark and cool in here.

What's that smell? It is kind of rich and earthy. As your eyes adjust to the darkness, you notice the ferns, gingers, herbs, and other small plants growing all around you. You bend down to tie your shoelace, and the forest floor appears to be moving. Upon closer inspection you discover insects galore—crawling millipedes, creeping centipedes, scampering beetles, hungry termites, scurrying ants, and even squishy earthworms.

Even though the soil looks rich, it is really not very fertile because the rain washes most of the soil's nutrients away. The insects eat the decaying plants and dead animals, allowing nutrients to be quickly recycled into the forest soil. Rain forest trees have shallow roots that enable them to use these nutrients efficiently.

Lost in the Wild *(cont.)*

Suddenly, a frog lands in front of you. Sidestepping the frog, you are careful not to step on the long, long column of army ants marching across the forest floor, looking for their next meal. Look to your right at that parade of leaves. Looking closely, you will discover that the moving carpet is really leaf-cutter ants carrying their bounty off to their underground nests. The leaves will become part of their home-grown fungus garden.

While intently engrossed in the leaf-cutter ant's activity, you fail to notice the monstrous vine-like stilt roots of a nearby tree. Tripping and falling to the forest floor, you land on a soft bed of ferns just as a giant anaconda slithers by.

Looking up, you become aware of the next layer of the rain forest called the understory. The large green leaves growing in this dimly lit layer make this an unbelievable emerald world. The dim light makes you realize that densely growing enormous leaves make it difficult for the sunlight to stream through. The plants here are happily growing in this shady environment.

As you focus on the giant leaves far above you, a screeching spider monkey lazily hangs by its tail, munching on a leaf, staring back at you. In yet another tree, you see a slow moving green blob. You realize it is the unusual sloth. You excitedly recognize that this is a mother sloth with its baby hanging from its belly.

You are distracted by a whooshing sound high above your head. Following the sound with your eyes, you see a swiftly swooping harpy eagle. It seems to be headed straight for the sloth. You frantically jump up and down and wave your hands in an effort to avert the eagle's attention. Luckily, it works! But now the eagle is after you. The howls of a howler monkey distract the eagle yet again. The howler monkey is able to hide among the dense foliage of the understory, and the eagle goes back to the emergent layer in frustration.

After all this excitement, you are tired and know you need to head for home. Even though you have explored only a small portion of the rain forest, your mind is filled with the sights and sounds of this emerald world. You look forward to coming back another day to continue your explorations.

Activity

- Draw your favorite part of the story.

- Use a 5 inch by 7 inch (13 cm by 18 cm) index card to design a postcard of your trip to the jungle. One side of the card should have a colored picture of what you saw. The other side should be divided in half. On one half write your message and on the other half put the address of the person to whom you are sending the postcard.

Walk on the Wild Side

A syllogism is a logical form of reasoning. It consists of three parts: a major premise, a minor premise, and a conclusion. *In any valid syllogism, the conclusion must be in agreement with and based upon the premises.* For example: All dogs can bark. (major premise) Petey is a dog. (minor premise) Therefore, Petey can bark. (conclusion)

Put a V on the line if the argument is valid or an I on the line if the argument is invalid.

_____ 1. A. All aye-ayes live in Madagascar.
    B. April is an aye-aye.
    C. Therefore, April lives in Madagascar.

_____ 2. A. All rain forest emergent layer trees have either stilt roots or buttress roots.
    B. The mahogany tree is found in the emergent layer of the rain forest.
    C. Therefore, mahogany trees have either stilt roots or buttress roots.

_____ 3. A. Many products found in the rain forest are useful as medicines.
    B. Tea is a product from the rain forest.
    C. Therefore, tea is a medicine.

_____ 4. A. Many bats eat nectar.
    B. Hummingbirds eat nectar.
    C. Therefore, hummingbirds are bats.

_____ 5. A. All orchid plants have flowers.
    B. The vanilla bean is an orchid.
    C. Therefore, the vanilla bean has flowers.

_____ 6. A. All poison-arrow frogs live in trees.
    B. Monkeys live in trees.
    C. Therefore, monkeys are poison-arrow frogs.

_____ 7. A. All animals who live in trees are called arboreal.
    B. Toucans live in trees.
    C. Therefore, toucans are arboreal.

_____ 8. A. All apes come from the rain forest.
    B. Chimpanzees are apes.
    C. Therefore, chimpanzees come from the rain forest.

_____ 9. A. Many forms of insects live in the rain forest.
    B. Flies are insects.
    C. Therefore, flies live in the rain forest.

_____ 10. A. All rosy periwinkle plants are found only in the rain forests of Madagascar.
    B. Rosy periwinkle plants are used to treat certain forms of cancer.
    C. Therefore, some cancer treatments come from Madagascar.

Raise a Rain Forest

Activity

Using these simple materials, you can make your own miniature rain forest and observe how it creates its own "rain."

Materials:

- clean, dry glass jar with lid (for example, a mayonnaise jar)
- potting soil
- gravel
- charcoal (the kind you would use in an aquarium)
- small rain forest plants or mosses (for example: prayer plant, philodendron, aluminum plant, begonia, peperomia, artillary plant)
- spoon

The air inside the jar gets recycled as the plants absorb the carbon dioxide and give off oxygen during the day. At night, the plants turn the oxygen back into carbon dioxide. The plants also recycle water by absorbing water from the soil and sending it up into the leaves. The leaves send the water back into the air as vapor. The water vapors turn into water droplets in the closed jar. It "rains" over and over again as the water droplets trickle back into the soil. Enjoy watching your own mini rain forest in action.

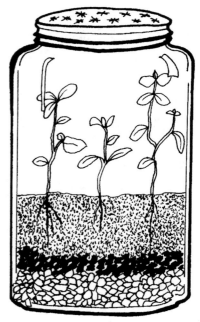

Directions:

1. Spread a layer of gravel on the bottom of the empty jar.
2. Add a layer of charcoal to the jar.
3. Add approximately 2 inches (5 cm) of soil.
4. Place the plants in the soil, making sure the roots are covered.
5. Water the soil to dampen. Do not soak.
6. Place the lid on the jar and keep it out of direct sunlight.
7. Jar lids may be decorated.

Challenge:

- Draw a diagram of your miniature rain forest. Show the various steps in the "rain" cycle and label the contents of the rain forest jar.

- As you observe the "rain" cycle in your miniature rain forest, keep a daily journal. Write entries about the changes you see occuring.

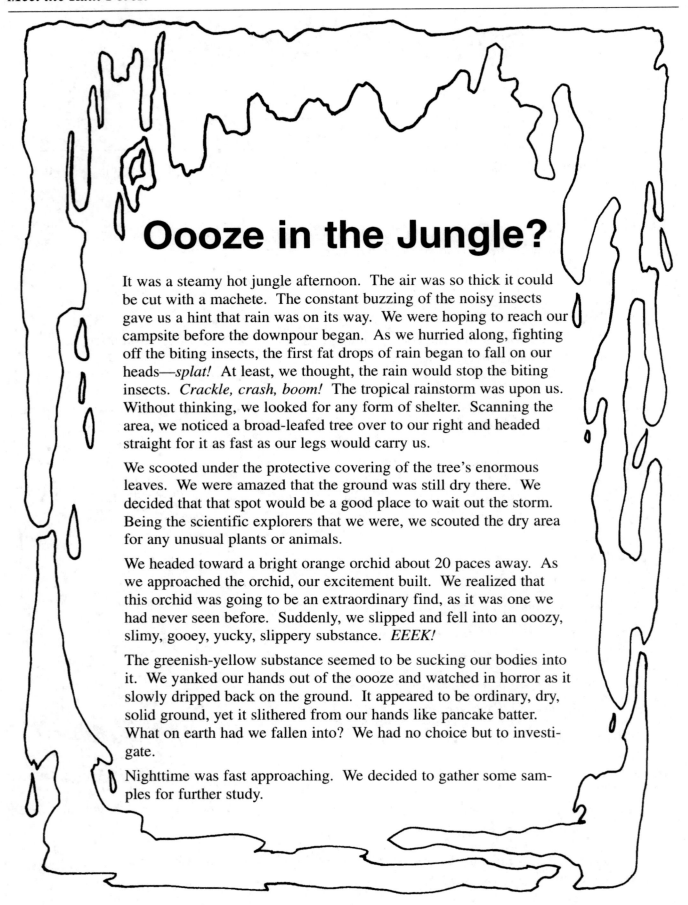

Oooze in the Jungle?

It was a steamy hot jungle afternoon. The air was so thick it could be cut with a machete. The constant buzzing of the noisy insects gave us a hint that rain was on its way. We were hoping to reach our campsite before the downpour began. As we hurried along, fighting off the biting insects, the first fat drops of rain began to fall on our heads—*splat!* At least, we thought, the rain would stop the biting insects. *Crackle, crash, boom!* The tropical rainstorm was upon us. Without thinking, we looked for any form of shelter. Scanning the area, we noticed a broad-leafed tree over to our right and headed straight for it as fast as our legs would carry us.

We scooted under the protective covering of the tree's enormous leaves. We were amazed that the ground was still dry there. We decided that that spot would be a good place to wait out the storm. Being the scientific explorers that we were, we scouted the dry area for any unusual plants or animals.

We headed toward a bright orange orchid about 20 paces away. As we approached the orchid, our excitement built. We realized that this orchid was going to be an extraordinary find, as it was one we had never seen before. Suddenly, we slipped and fell into an ooozy, slimy, gooey, yucky, slippery substance. *EEEK!*

The greenish-yellow substance seemed to be sucking our bodies into it. We yanked our hands out of the oooze and watched in horror as it slowly dripped back on the ground. It appeared to be ordinary, dry, solid ground, yet it slithered from our hands like pancake batter. What on earth had we fallen into? We had no choice but to investigate.

Nighttime was fast approaching. We decided to gather some samples for further study.

Oooze in the Jungle? *(cont.)*

Activity

This lesson is a scientific investigation of the properties of oooze.

Materials: (for each two groups of four to six students)

- newspaper (a lot)
- 1 large mixing bowl
- mixing spoon
- water
- 1 small bottle yellow or green food coloring
- 1 (16 oz/454 g) box of cornstarch (a little extra cornstarch may be needed to adjust consistency)
- 2 aluminum pie plates (or other type of shallow container)
- large piece of paper to chart results
- marker

Teacher Directions:

1. Prepare oooze about 45 minutes before presenting lesson to allow it to settle and to ensure proper consistency.

2. Into two cups (500 mL) of water add four to five drops of food coloring and stir. Add one box of cornstarch. Swirl and tip the bowl to level the contents. Put bowl aside for contents to settle.

3. After about fifteen minutes, mix the oooze by hand to ensure even consistency. Lift the oooze from the bottom of the bowl to the top by slipping your fingers under it until an even consistency is reached.

   Please Note: Oooze should flow when you tip the bowl, but feel like a solid when you run your finger across the surface. If it is too thick to flow, add a little water. If it is too runny, add a little more cornstarch. Some water will evaporate after prolonged use, so additional water may be necessary.

4. Read the story "Oooze in the Jungle?" to the class.

5. Discuss with the students that preliminary investigation has proven that the oooze is safe to handle even though we are not certain about its composition.

6. Explain to the students that their job is to investigate the properties of oooze. A property of a substance is something that can be seen, heard, smelled, touched, or detected by instruments (like a microscope). The color, size, shape, texture, weight, hardness, odor, and sound of a substance are examples of its properties.

7. Divide the class into investigation teams of four to six students each.

Oooze in the Jungle? *(cont.)*

Activity *(cont.)*

8. Cover the work area with multiple layers of newspaper. You may choose to spread some on the floor also. (Oooze, however, can be swept up or vacuumed when it dries.)

9. Distribute equal amounts of oooze to each team in the aluminum pie plates. Allow the students some time to use their senses to investigate the oooze. They should use all their senses except their sense of taste.

10. Give each team a large piece of paper and a marker. Ask each team to choose a recorder. The recorder should wash his/her hands before recording.

11. After each group discussion of the properties of oooze, the recorder should list at least five properties.

12. To assist the students in their investigations, ask the following questions:

    • How does oooze behave when you press on it?

    • When does oooze behave like a solid?

    • When does oooze behave like a liquid?

Students may conclude that oooze becomes liquid due to body heat. Suggest that they test that theory by putting the oooze on various objects, for example, a piece of plastic or wood.

13. Explain to the students the importance of experimentation or testing to solve a disagreement about a property.

14. Each group will post their completed charts and present their findings to the class.

15. Discuss the similarities and differences of each group's findings.

Cleanup Directions:

1. Save the bowls of oooze until the next day so that the students can see what it looks like when it dries.

2. Oooze can be reconstituted by adding some water and mixing.

3. Dry oooze can be disposed of by simply dumping it into a wastebasket.

4. **DO NOT POUR OOOZE DOWN THE SINK. IT WILL CLOG THE DRAIN!**

Challenge:

• Create your own story about the origins of oooze.

Sensory Writing

Using your senses, write a two to three page story describing what it *smells, feels, sounds,* and *looks* like in a rain forest. Include illustrations.

Use a large piece of colored construction paper as a folder for your story. Color and cut out the picture below. Then glue it to your front cover as a decoration.

_____

(Title)

by _____

Biodiversity

Biodiversity refers to the differences that exist among all living things. Nowhere else on earth, except for the tropical coral reefs, is life more abundant than in tropical rain forests. If you combined all of the tropical rain forests that still exist, they would contain at least half of the world's species, even though the rain forests cover less than six percent of the land's surface.

There is a greater diversity of plant and animal species found in the rain forests of Panama than found on the entire continent of Europe. More species of fish can be found in the Amazon River of Brazil than in all of the rivers of the United States combined.

Research in the tropical jungles has given us new information concerning the number of species found on earth. A few years ago scientists believed that there were between five and ten million species globally. Now, after scientific exploration of the tropical canopy, the total number of species is believed to be closer to 30 million!

Why is there so much diversity found in the jungle? The varied layers of the rain forest provide a great variety of habitats for diverse species. Between the forest floor and the towering emergent layer, there is a vast difference in rainfall, temperature, and sunlight. It is these varying conditions between the layers which enable the many different species to flourish.

Believe It or Not...

- Two-thirds of all flowering plants are found in tropical rain forests.

- There are 103 different types of bats found in Costa Rica.

- Columbian rain forests have 1,400 different bird species.

- In just one acre of the Borneo rain forest, there are seven hundred different kinds of trees.

- Forty-three different kinds of ants can be found living on one rain forest tree in Peru.

Activity I

Choose a small area on the school grounds where you would like to conduct a study of biodiversity. Use either chalk or string to identify the boundaries of each area of study. List and tally all living things that are found within the assigned space. Use of a magnifying glass is suggested. Repeat this activity at least twice more on different days and at different times to obtain a more accurate account of the biodiversity of your chosen area.

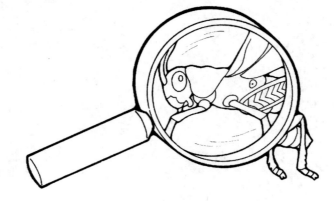

Graph your results, using a bar graph or a pictograph. Then classify your results into categories. Finally, compare your results from each day on a line graph.

Biodiversity *(cont.)*

The purpose of this activity is to provide an understanding that the destruction of even a small section of a rain forest can result in the extinction of many species.

Materials:

- one biodiversity chart for each group (page 24)
- one bag of jelly beans (various colors) for each group
- pencils

Directions:

The Biodiversity Chart on page 24 represents the rain forest. The different colors of jelly beans represent the many species found there. Each color of jelly bean will represent one species found in the rain forest.

1. Divide the class into groups of three to four students. Give each group a small bag of different colored jelly beans.

2. Have each group randomly pour its bag of jelly beans onto the gridded chart. Any jelly beans that fall outside the grids are not counted.

3. Choose one member of each group to count the number of species (jelly beans) in its rain forest. Record this number.

4. Destroy part of the rain forest by removing the jelly beans in grid number one. Count and record the number of different species left in the rain forest. Have any species become endangered or extinct yet?

5. Take turns destroying the rain forest (removing the jelly beans) one grid at a time. Count and record the number of different species still remaining after the destruction of each section.

6. How much rain forest was destroyed before the first species became extinct? Record the number of sections destroyed on the chart.

7. How much rain forest was destroyed before one half of the species became extinct? Record the number of sections destroyed on the chart. Have groups compare results.

8. What does this activity teach us about the importance of preserving the rain forest? Even if a small area of rain forest is destroyed, an entire species might become extinct.

9. This activity can be repeated using different grid sizes. Does this change the results?

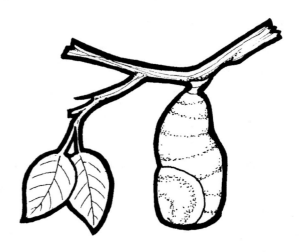

Biodiversity *(cont.)*

1	2	3	4
5	6	7	8
9	10	11	12
13	14	15	16

Total number of species in the rain forest: _____

Species remaining after destroying . . .

Grid 1 _____   Grid 5 _____   Grid 9 _____   Grid 13_____

Grid 2 _____   Grid 6 _____   Grid 10_____   Grid 14_____

Grid 3 _____   Grid 7 _____   Grid 11_____   Grid 15_____

Grid 4 _____   Grid 8 _____   Grid 12_____   Grid 16_____

How much rain forest was destroyed before the first species became extinct?

_____ **grids were destroyed.**

When half of the species became extinct, _____ **grids (sections of the rain forest) were destroyed.**

Hidden Rain Forest Words

How many words can you create from the word...

Biodiversity

_____   _____   _____   _____

_____   _____   _____   _____

_____   _____   _____   _____

_____   _____   _____   _____

_____   _____   _____   _____

_____   _____   _____   _____

_____   _____   _____   _____

_____   _____   _____   _____

_____   _____   _____   _____

_____   _____   _____   _____

_____   _____   _____   _____

_____   _____   _____   _____

_____   _____   _____   _____

_____   _____   _____   _____

Challenge: Write a story using as many of these words as you can.

My Cup Runneth Over

Activity

Many rain forests are being destroyed each year because of the need for farmland and timber. The purpose of this scientific exploration is to demonstrate how the nutrients in the rain forest soil wash away quickly when the land is cleared.

Materials:

- 1 cup (250 mL) ordinary soil
- 1 cup (250 mL) sand
- 4 twelve-ounce (355 mL) clear plastic cups
- 1 cup (250 mL) torn leaves or fresh grass clippings
- 1 shallow aluminum pan about 9 inches by 12 inches (23 by 30 cm)
- 2 cups (500 mL) water
- scissors

Directions:

1. Mix the sand and the soil in the pan.
2. Use the point of the scissors to make ten small holes in the bottoms of two of the plastic cups.
3. Fill each cup one-half full with the sand/soil mixture. The soil represents nutrients that help plants grow.
4. Add a one-inch (2.5 cm) layer of leaves or grass to one of the cups filled with the mixture.
5. Place two empty cups into the aluminum pan.
6. Hold the two mixture-filled cups directly over the empty cups.
7. Pour water into each mixture-filled cup until full.
8. Observe mixture-filled cups and collection cups. What is happening?
9. How does this scientific exploration relate to cutting down the rain forests?

Explanation:

Water flows quickly through the cup without grass or leaves, making the collection cup muddier. Where rain forests have been cleared, the soil washes away when it rains because there are no roots to hold it in place. This rain forest soil collects in the rivers, which causes them to clog up with silt. The Amazon River in Brazil is so full of mud that many of the animals that live in this very dark environment have lost their eyesight because they no longer have a need for it. Furthermore, during heavy tropical rains, the rivers cannot absorb all of the falling rain, and flooding occurs.

Life in the Tropical Rain Forest — Animals

This section focuses on the diversity of rain forest life, how plants and animals adapt, and the interaction of the rain forest animals with their environment.

Endangered Animals

There are more endangered animals today than ever before. The activities in the following section will not only help you understand more about these animals but also show you ways to help save them.

Suggestions for Extending the Section

1. Animal Information Cards and Animal Illustration Cards may be mounted on construction paper and used in a learning center.

2. Write a research paper. Animals very close to becoming extinct are called *endangered*. Animals close to becoming endangered are called *threatened*. Research an endangered rain forest animal making sure to include:

   - Physical description
   - Diet
   - Environment
   - Natural enemies
   - Unusual characteristics
   - Why this animal has become endangered

   Use your information in either a written or oral report. Make sure that you use visual aids in your presentation.

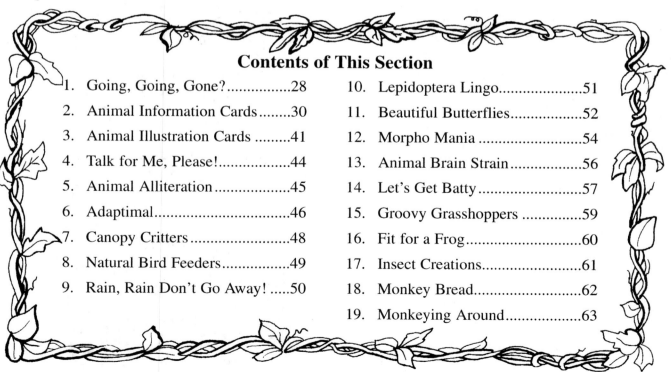

Contents of This Section

Going, Going, Gone?

Many vertebrate animals (animals with backbones) that live in the tropical rain forests are in danger of becoming extinct. Vertebrate animals can be divided into the five groups represented below:

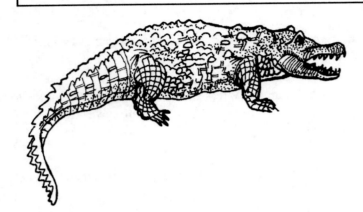

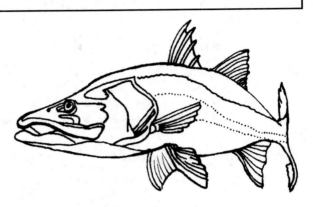

Reptiles: cold-blooded, have scales, breathe air with lungs

Fish: cold-blooded, live in water, breathe with gills, have scales on skin

Amphibians: cold-blooded, born in water, babies have gills, adults have lungs, live on land as adults

Birds: warm-blooded, have wings, most have feathers, most fly

Mammals: warm-blooded, have hair, give birth to live young, babies feed on mothers' milk

28

Going, Going, Gone? *(cont.)*

Each of the rain forest animals listed below is either endangered or threatened. Write the name of each animal under the vertebrate group to which it belongs.

Puerto Rican Boa	Howler Monkey	Jaguar
Aye-Aye	Radiated Tortoise	Indigo Macaw
Leopard	Arapaima Fish	Red-Necked Parrot
Panamanian Golden Frog	Giant Anteater	African Dwarf Crocodile
Monte Verde Toad	Tree Sloth	Chimpanzee
Giant Orangutan	Giant Catfish	Harpy Eagle

Birds

_____

_____

_____

Reptiles

_____

_____

_____

Amphibians

_____

_____

Fish

_____

_____

Mammals

_____

_____

_____

_____

_____

_____

Animal Information Cards

Guide to Using the Cards

Pages 30–40 are filled with Animal Information Cards. These boxes may be mounted on colored construction paper and be placed on the classroom walls. Pages 41–43 have the corresponding Animal Illustration Cards. These may also be mounted and displayed adjacent to the appropriate Information Cards.

The Animal Information and Illustration Cards can also be used in a matching game. For example, post the information cards around the room. Read the descriptions, one at a time, to the class. Allow one student to match the correct illustration to the Information Card.

These cards can provide an excellent, initial resource if you are having your students do animal research reports. At the end of this section, there are some blank cards for research of other rain forest animals.

Challenge: The following are challenge questions and activites related to some selected animals on the Animal Information Cards. You might use these as extra credit, quiz questions, or discussion starting points.

Parrots: Research how parrots can be bred humanely in captivity. Would you buy a parrot bred this way for a pet? Why or why not?

Harpy Eagle: Being a predator, the harpy eagle is an integral part of the balance of nature in the tropical rain forest. What do you think would happen if this predator became extinct?

Sloth: If a sloth moves through the branches at only one-half mile per hour, how long would it take for him to travel to the next cecropia tree six miles away?

Jaguar: Compare and contrast the plight of the jaguar with that of the leopard.

Chimpanzees: Write a commercial for a tool from a chimp's point of view. Perform your commercial for your class.

Quetzal

The quetzal of Southern Mexico and Central America is among the most beautiful birds in the world. The quetzal is also known as the royal bird of Costa Rica. Its body is green with highlights of gold and red. The black wings of the quetzal have splashes of white on them. The male quetzal is about 15 inches (38 cm) in length from head to tail. However, the long wisp of feathers beneath its tail add another 15 to 30 inches (38 to 76 cm) to the quetzal's length. The female quetzal is slightly less attractive. Her feathers are not as vibrant in color nor are her feathers as long and graceful as her male counterpart's.

Quetzals are known to eat ants and wasps, but they mainly depend on the fruits of the wild avocado tree for nourishment. The quetzal is an endangered animal because excessive logging of the rain forest has resulted in the loss of many wild avocado trees.

The quetzal's great beauty has inspired people to incorporate it into their cultures in many ways. Often, rain forest native art and mythology have featured this royal bird. The ancient Mayans and Aztecs considered the quetzal to be a sacred creature. Today, the quetzal serves as the national symbol of Guatemala.

Animal Information Cards *(cont.)*

Macaw

Macaws are the world's largest parrots. There are several different kinds of spectacularly colored macaws, and they all live in South America. Macaws are seed predators rather than seed dispersers. They are able to eat the toughest fruits and seeds, even if they contain toxic chemicals.

Macaws have large, powerful bodies which protect them from being eaten by many bird predators. The macaw's hooked beak can open even the hardest nuts, like Brazil nuts, with ease. It uses the edge of the beak like a saw to cut partially through the shell, making it easy to complete the job. The top and bottom parts of the macaw's beak constantly rub against each other, keeping the edges sharp.

The macaw's beak is also useful as an extra foot when climbing through the trees. The macaw's foot has four toes. Two of these face forward, and two of them face backward. This enables the macaws to pick up objects and hold them tightly.

Parrots, such as macaws, make popular pets and are often taken into captivity. Although there are laws attempting to protect the parrots, poachers continue to illegally capture and sell these beautiful creatures.

Toucan

Some of the most distinctive birds that come from the tropical rain forests are toucans. Toucans have large, brightly colored beaks which are serrated and are displayed in courtship rituals. Toucan beaks are so large that they are sometimes longer than the toucan's body!

There are about 37 species of toucans, the largest of which is the Ramphastos. In general, the toucan's body is usually one to two feet (30 to 60 cm) in length. The plumage of these birds match their personalities; both are very loud. Sections of the vibrant colors such as red, yellow, and green contrast sharply with the mostly black or dark green feathers on the toucan's body. These colorful birds are supported by strong legs and feet which have two toes pointed forward and two toes pointed backward.

Toucans nest in the tree cavities of the Central and South American rain forests. In these nests, both toucan parents incubate and raise their offspring. Fruit makes up the bulk of the toucan diet.

Animal Information Cards *(cont.)*

Harpy Eagle

The topical rain forest is the home to the world's largest and most ferocious eagle, the harpy eagle. This rare predator hunts high up in the jungle canopy. It sleeps at night and hunts by day. The harpy eagle is a very swift and agile flyer which enables it to chase monkeys through the jungle. Its gray feathers provide the eagle with a natural camouflage.

The harpy eagle makes its nest in the tallest emergent trees (most often the silk cotton trees). Usually only one harpy eagle chick is successfully raised on the large platform of twigs used as a nest. It takes six months for the chick to reach adulthood.

The harpy eagle dines mainly on unsuspecting, sleeping sloths and chattering capuchin monkeys. Occasionally, their diet includes agouti, kinkajous, snakes, anteaters, large parrots, and small deer.

Caiman

Caimans are reptiles that are closely related to their Central and South American neighbors, the alligators. Adult caimans are usually four to six feet (1.8 m) in length. They have short legs and powerful tails which are used for both swimming and as weapons.

Caimans live along river banks where they patiently wait for thirsty animals to come for a drink—then, they attack their unsuspecting prey! They can float under the water with only their eyes, nostrils, and ears showing. A valve closes off the gullet of the windpipe so that the mouth can be opened under water to eat its favorite food—fish. The caiman's greatest enemy is Man.

Some caimans have been found to leave the river to lay their eggs next to termite nests. As the termites continue to build their nest, they surround the caiman's eggs. The nests keep half the eggs warm and half the eggs cool. The warm eggs develop into male caimans, and the cool eggs develop into females. When the baby caimans hatch, they head straight for the river where they spend their lives.

Animal Information Cards *(cont.)*

Gorilla

Because gorillas are the largest living primates, they are quite often misunderstood. They are usually represented as aggressive, violent, and short-tempered creatures, when in fact they are actually one of the most gentle primates in existence. These giants of the African rain forests can reach up to six feet (180 cm) in height and 400 pounds (180 kg) in weight. Despite their size, fighting among the gorillas is rare.

Contrary to popular belief, the gorillas are not carnivores (meat eaters), but rather they are herbivores (plant eaters). During the daytime they forage for food on the forest floor. Unlike other members of the Ape family, most gorillas, due to their size, do not scour the tree tops in search of food or shelter.

Gorillas live and travel in family groupings. The family unit consists of one dominate silverback male (the term "silverback" comes from the gray fur on a mature male), one or two females, a few young males, and various juveniles. Gorillas are quadrupeds because they travel on all four limbs. They use the knuckles of their hands to help support their heavy upper bodies.

Tarsier

The tarsier lives in the rain forests of Indonesia, Malaysia, Brunei, and the Philippines. This Southeast Asian mammal is in danger of extinction because its forests are being destroyed. The tarsier is a rat-sized relative of the monkey.

This creature is one of the strangest looking primates, in large part because of its unique eyes, ears, and feet. Its body is only about six inches (15 cm) in length. The tarsier has long, powerful hind legs which allow it to leap up to 20 feet (6 meters). The pads on their toes and fingers help them to hold on to branches. The tarsier's head can almost turn in a complete circle. This is a very important feature, since the tarsier cannot move its eyes.

This animal spends most of its life living in the trees of the rain forest. It is, for the most part, nocturnal (active during the night and resting during the day) and it has large, sharp eyes that enable it to hunt all sorts of small animals at night. It leaps onto its prey (which is usually a lizard or an insect), it catches the creature with its hands, and then kills it with its sharp teeth.

Animal Information Cards *(cont.)*

Fer-de-lance

The most feared poisonous snake found in Central and South America is called the fer-de-lance. This snake gets its name from the Creole-French language and it means "head of a lance." A lance is a type of weapon that has a spearhead, which some people believe looks similar to the head of this snake. The fer-de-lance averages four to six feet (1.2 to 1.8 meters) in length but can grow up to seven feet (2.1 meters) long. Usually olive or dark brown in color, it has a pattern of dark-edged triangles on its skin.

Small depressions on its head mark a heat-sensing organ that helps the animal find its warm-blooded, mammalian prey by the heat the prey generates. The fer-de-lance protects itself by striking its enemy. Its venom quickly produces severe hemorrhaging and is lethal.

This snake lives in the understory or forest floor, hiding among the leaf litter, tree roots, and buttresses. It gives birth to live offspring and may produce as many as 70 young at one time.

Boa

Boas are nonpoisonous snakes. They kill their food by wrapping themselves around an animal and squeezing tightly until the animal dies from suffocation. Boas then stretch their jaws open extremely wide to swallow their prey whole. They are able to open their jaws so wide that they can actually swallow animals that are larger than their own heads.

There are about 70 species in the boa family which can be found worldwide. Unlike some other types of snakes who lay eggs, the boa gives birth to live offspring. Some kinds of boas never grow any longer than 24 inches (61 cm), while others, such as the boa constrictor, may grow as large as 14 feet (4 meters) in length.

One of the most beautiful snakes found in Central and South America is the emerald tree boa. Its green skin is striped with white or yellow, which camouflages it well in its home in the canopy layer. This protective coloration allows the snake to approach its prey without being seen and also helps it to avoid being eaten by its predators, one of which is the harpy eagle.

Animal Information Cards *(cont.)*

Lemur

Lemurs are distant cousins of monkeys. They are found only on the island of Madagascar. They have been able to survive there because of a lack of monkeys on the island that would be competing for the same food.

There are 15 different kinds of lemurs in Madagascar. Most of them are cat or squirrel-sized but some, like the mouse lemur, are as small as five inches (12.7 cm) long and weigh only two ounces (56 g). The indri lemur is the biggest lemur, growing to over two feet (61 m) long. It is able to make extraordinary leaps through the trees but, when on the ground, bounces on its big back legs.

Most lemurs roam the forest in small groups looking for food. They eat fruit, leaves, bark and insects. Different types of lemurs are active during different times of the day. Some species are nocturnal (active at night), some are diurnal (active during the day), and some are active only at dusk.

The lemur population is dwindling. Some species of lemurs are in danger of extinction because the forests of Madagascar are rapidly being destroyed.

Aye-aye

The cat-sized aye-aye is an unusual and rare type of lemur. Its enormous eyes and rounded, hairless ears indicate that the aye-aye is nocturnal (it comes out at night). During the daytime it sleeps in hollow trees or among branches. The aye-aye is a very small animal, measuring only about 36 inches (.91 m) long; more than half of that length is due to its bushy tail.

The aye-aye is a loner. It hunts alone, using its long fingers to scoop out bamboo pith, sugar cane, beetles, and insect larvae. The curved, slender fingers are also used to comb its fur. Unfortunately for the aye-aye, the natives of Madagascar believe that these long fingers possess magical properties and bring good luck to the owners. Many aye-ayes have lost their lives because of this—their fingers did not bring them good luck!

Aye-ayes can be found only on the island of Madagascar, and there are fewer than ten aye-ayes known to exist there. Aye-ayes are not found in any of the world's zoos; therefore, the only way we will probably ever view one is to look in a book.

Animal Information Cards *(cont.)*

Orangutan

Orangutans can be found only on the islands of Borneo and Sumatra in Southeast Asia. They were named "men of the woods" because their faces are so human-looking. Orangutans are wonderful climbers and spend most of their time in the treetops, swinging from branch to branch.

Like other apes, orangutans do not have tails. They have long red hair and strong arms. Their long toes help them grip the branches as they climb in the trees.

Orangutans have huge appetites. Their favorite food is fruit, but they will also eat leaves, shoots, tree bark and, occasionally, birds' eggs. Orangutans are very clever and have learned to follow fruit-eating birds to find their favorite food.

The orangutans have become very rare due to the loss of their habitat, the rain forest. Additionally, orangutans have been hunted, captured, and sold as pets. Special reserves have been set up to help the remaining orangutans survive.

Indian Elephant

Indian elephants are the largest animals in the rain forests of Asia, although their African cousins are larger. Elephants roam about in small herds. Their diet mainly consists of leaves, which they pull from the trees and shove into their mouths using their trunks.

The Indian elephant's two very large teeth are called tusks. These tusks consist of ivory. The females usually have smaller tusks than the males. Unlike the flat back of the African elephant, the Indian elephant has a strongly arched back. It has a domed forehead and a smooth trunk. It can weigh up to six tons (5.44 tonnes). The ears of the Indian elephant do not reach down as far as its mouth and are smaller than the ears of the African elephant.

Indian elephants have been trained as workers in the forests. They are better than machines when it comes to getting out big logs from between the trees. They can drag huge logs from the forest and pick them up with their trunks and tusks. The forests where they live are gradually being destroyed, and the irony of it is that the tamed, working elephants are helping to cause the damage.

Animal Information Cards *(cont.)*

Anteater

This tree-living, cat-sized anteater is also called a tamandua. It has short, coarse fur and a prehensile tail. South American tamanduas have honey-colored coats, while the Central American ones have bold, two-toned black and tan coats.

The tamandua has powerful claws that help it both in climbing and in getting food. It wraps its tail around tree limbs to hold on while it rips open ant and termite nests with its claws. It then catches the insects with its long sticky tongue, licking up thousands at one time. It also will eat other insects such as bees and beetles.

Contrary to common belief, the anteater does not eat all types of ants or termites! They avoid army ants because the are too aggressive and can sting. It also will not eat leaf cutter ants, as they are spiny and difficult to swallow in its long, toothless mouth. Azteca ants are a favorite of the tamandua, but the anteaters approach these nests very cautiously. After several minutes of eating these azteca ants, thousands more of them pour out from the nest, covering the tamandua and biting it with their tiny jaws, causing the tamandua to retreat.

Agouti

The agouti is a large, rabbit-sized rodent with a short tail and long legs. It is mainly active by day (diurnal), but is also active at dusk or at night (nocturnal). It lives on the forest floor and sleeps in burrows.

Agoutis have a very strange behavior called scatter-hoarding. Most rodents destroy all the seeds that they gather and eat; the agouti, however, carries seeds long distances and buries them whole.

There are some trees that produce seeds that are too heavy to be dispersed by bats or monkeys and have to rely on animals like agoutis for dispersal. Brazil nut fruits fall to the ground where their hard, woody shells are chiseled open by the agouti.

The agouti eats some of the seeds and scatter-hoard the rest. They do not usually find all the Brazil nut seeds that they bury; consequently, these seeds germinate and grow into new Brazil nut trees.

Animal Information Cards *(cont.)*

Sloth

The sloth does nearly everything upside down. Found in Central and South America, this slowest-of-all-mammals' top speed is one-half mile per hour. It lives its entire life in one cecropia tree, hanging by its huge hook-like claws. In addition to cecropia leaves, it eats flowers, fruit, and insects.

Its long, coarse, grayish-brown fur grows from its belly towards it back (the opposite of all other animals' fur), which enables the rain to run off easily, keeping the sloth dry in the wet rain forest. Nonetheless, its fur often appears a greenish color due to the algae that grow on it. In addition to the algae, the sloth's fur contains sloth moths, beetles, and mites. When the sloth descends to the forest floor, these insects utilize the sloth's dung to lay their eggs. Caterpillars also live on the sloth's fur and feed on the algae.

The sloth spends nearly its entire life among the tree's branches. It visits the forest floor about once every week or two to defecate, thereby fertilizing its own home. Once on the ground, the sloth cannot walk and must drag itself. However, during the rainy season, when the Amazon floods, sloths can swim from tree top to tree top.

Jaguar

The rarely seen jaguar is the largest predator of the dense forests of Central and South America. The jaguar is an excellent swimmer and climber and usually can be found close to water, where it sleeps by day and hunts by night (a nocturnal animal). It prefers to eat large animals like wild pig or tapir, but, being an excellent hunter, its diet also includes sloths, snakes, mice, caimans, turtles, iguanas, and fish. The jaguar is the major predator of the lower levels of the rain forest.

The jaguar's coat is spotted like its cousin's, the leopard, but its rings are different. Nearly all of them have a spot in the middle. This camouflages the jaguar as he stalks through the jungle. Jaguars can weigh up to three hundred pounds (136 kg).

A number of disasters threaten these beautiful creatures. Jaguars have long been hunted for their luxurious fur. Although there are many laws protecting these creatures, illegal killing and smuggling of the jaguars' fur continues. As the population grows, rain forest land is being slashed and burned to clear land for ranching. This is causing a loss of habitat for many rain forest animals which the jaguar depends upon for food. Consequently, the jaguars have begun to feed on the ranchers' livestock. In turn, this has resulted in their being killed by the ranchers.

Animal Information Cards *(cont.)*

Chimpanzee

Scientists believe that of all wild animals, chimpanzees are our closest relative. Chimpanzees make their homes in the rain forests of Africa. They have been known to live in groups of up to 100 animals. The noisiest male is usually the group leader. Male chimpanzees often fight with one another. Female chimps are friendlier and get along well. Male chimps grow to be about five feet (1.52 m) tall and weigh about 110 pounds (50 kg). Female chimps are usually a little smaller. Chimps, like other apes, do not have tails.

Chimpanzees eat plants and meat. They are capable of killing pigs and antelope for food. Male chimps work in teams to trap monkeys in trees. When they are lucky enough to find a large amount of food, the males make drumming noises on the tree trunks to call other chimps to the feast.

Chimpanzees are very clever. They have learned how to use simple tools to get the food they want. They use sticks to crack nuts to get the juicy kernels inside and to catch tasty termites. Chimps have also been known to chew leaves, making them spongy, so they can use them to soak up water for drinking.

_____

(animal)

_____

_____

_____

_____

_____

_____

_____

Blank Cards

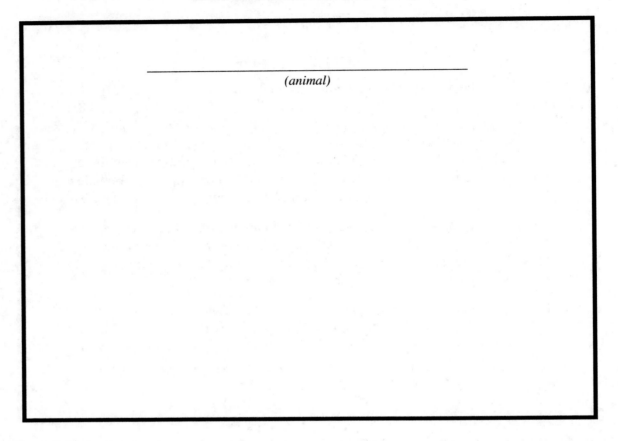

_____
(animal)

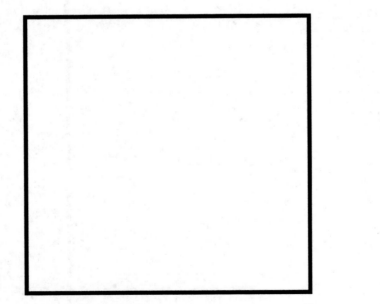

Animal Illustration Cards

Quetzal

Macaw

Toucan

Harpy Eagle

Caiman

Gorilla

Animal Illustration Cards *(cont.)*

Tarsier

Fer-de-Lance

Boa

Lemur

Aye-aye

Orangutan

Animal Illustration Cards *(cont.)*

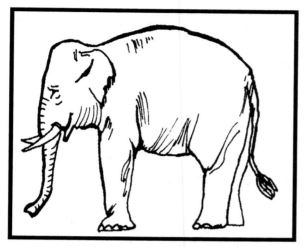

Indian Elephant

Anteater

Agouti

Sloth

Jaguar

Chimpanzee

Talk for Me, Please!

If you were one of the endangered rain forest animals you have read about, what would you tell people about your problems (for example: disappearing habitat, lack of food, etc.)? Write this in a letter form and remember to include how the person you are writing to can help to preserve your way of life.

_____

_____

_____
(your address and date)

_____

_____

_____
(recipient's name and address)

_____
(greeting)

_____

_____

_____

_____

_____

_____
(closing)

_____
(signature)

Animal Alliteration

Alliteration is the repetition of the same sound at the beginning of each word in a sentence or phrase. **Example:**

Six slimy snakes slithered slowly.

Four fat frogs froze from fright.

Activity

On your own or with a partner write a four-to six-line poem about a tropical rain forest animal using alliteration. (Challenge yourself by trying to rhyme the even-numbered lines.)

_____

(animal)

_____

_____

_____

_____

_____

Now that you have completed your alliteration poem, write a quatrain (a four-line poem) with an ABAB rhyming pattern. Remember to use the same beginning sound as often as possible. Use the back of this paper.

Adaptimal

(Adapt an Animal)

Many species of animals are becoming endangered due to loss of habitat. All living things need a place to live, to find food, and to carry on all other life-sustaining functions.

What do you think would happen to an animal if an important part of its habitat were destroyed?

If an animal is to survive in a changing environment, it must adapt or change its behaviors. It may take many generations for an animal to make adaptive changes. The best chance of survival for an animal is to live in a very diverse habitat.

Activity

Create an imaginary rain forest animal fighting for survival in a changing environment. Changes in the rain forest have altered its habitat. These changes would have endangered most other animals. Make the "adaptimal" victorious in its struggle to survive.

Directions:

Using the cartoon frames provided on page 47, create a cartoon story about how this "adaptimal" fights for survival in its changing environment and eventually succeeds.

1. In the first frame, draw a cartoon of the "adaptimal" in its environment before it changed.

2. In the following frames, show the environmental changes and how the "adaptimal" deals with these changes.

3. In the last frame, show the new and improved "adaptimal" in its changed environment.

4. Keep in mind the most drastic adaptions made by animals in order to survive a changing habitat happen very slowly—sometimes over many years—even centuries.

Note: Due to the fact that it may take many generations for nature to perfect its adaptions, a threatened species may well be extinct before the changes occur.

Challenge:

1. Discuss the impact to an environment if an animal becomes extinct.

2. Would this affect other animals? How and why?

3. Do people have any responsibility in preventing an animal from becoming extinct?

Adaptimal Cartoon Frames

1	**2**
3	**4**
5	**6**

Canopy Critters

Circle the following words in the word search:

Agouti	Gibbon	Okapi	Tamandua
Anteater	Golden Cat	Opossum	Tapir
Armadillo	Gorilla	Orangutan	Tamarin
Bulldog Bat	Indris	Paca	Tarsier
Bushdog	Jaguar	Peccary	Tayra
Chimpanzee	Kinkajou	Porcupine	Tiger
Coatimundi	Lemur	Red Howler	Uakari
Deer	Long-Tongued Bat	Rhinoceros	Vampire Bat
Elephant	Mandrill	Shrew	Wooly Monkey
Flying Fox	Margay	Sloth	Wrinkle-Faced Bat
Gaur	Night Monkey	Spider Monkey	
Ghost Bat	Ocelot	Squirrel	

```
M V V Q A G Y X Z D G L E R R I U Q S W K
R T A M A R I N T P B A K I N K A J O U S
A M A R G A Y A A Y O D L J C B G O R V J
U V S B P D C B P N T R N L H L L I E Z X
G G A I D N U M I T A O C K I Y Z T C T B
A A O M E E S X R N B T E U M R C U O N U
J W U D P S C P O B D U U P U O O N A H E
B A L R H I V A I F X R N G A I A G I H L
A O G R E S R G F D G K I K N C N A H P L
G F E U T E U E P E E N A S Z A A E R E I
H W L O A A D B B Y L R I L E P R P T L R
O K T K C R B J W A I K M Y E S S O Q E D
S T A B D E U G N O T G N O L H S L D T N
T J M I Y E K N O M T H G I N F V H O I A
B T A R S I E R D D T I G E R K O L V T M
A A N T E A T E R I L Y O V F W E K A W H
T D D L Q A R M A D I L L O L C I Y A K P
O M U S S O P O B Y C I U E O J R W A P K
Y R A C C E P U L E M U R B A A U V M G I
```

Natural Bird Feeders

The secret of the rain forest is that its plants reuse almost everything that falls to the floor and decays there. The environment can be saved by reusing more and wasting less. Using our earth's natural resources with care is called *conservation*; reusing materials is called *recycling*. The following activity recycles pine cones into bird feeders.

Materials:

- 1 large pine cone
- peanut butter
- bird seed
- 24-inch (61 cm) piece of string
- plastic knife
- wax paper

Directions:

1. Cover work area with an appropriate-sized piece of wax paper.
2. Tie string around pine cone, leaving a loop as a hanger.
3. Spread peanut butter on large pine cone.
4. Generously sprinkle peanut butter with bird seed.
5. After the peanut butter dries, hang pine cone in a tree.
6. Enjoy observing the visiting birds to your natural bird feeder.

Another way to help the environment is to reuse and recycle man-made products. Instead of throwing away your next milk carton, try reusing it to create this bird feeder.

Materials:

- one quart (.95 liter) milk carton, empty
- bird seed
- string
- scissors

Directions:

1. Thoroughly wash the empty milk carton.
2. Cut a large, rectangular window on each side of the carton.
3. Fill the bottom of the carton with birdseed.
4. Cut a hole in the top of the carton and pull a string through it.
5. Decorate your carton if you wish.
6. Hang your bird feeder from a tree.

Rain, Rain, Don't Go Away!

Design a Slogan

To help make the public aware of the plight of our disappearing rain forests and the creatures that live there, design a slogan and illustration on the T-shirt pattern provided. Display these T-shirt slogans in a prominent place at your school.

Some examples of slogans are: "You Too Can Save the Toucan," "May the Forest Be with You," and "Save the Sloth and the Moth."

Challenge:

Contact a local T-shirt printing company and have your design printed on T-shirts. You could sell these as a fund raiser to save land in the rain forest.

Lepidoptera Lingo

Lepidoptera is the scientific term for moths and butterflies. The tropical rain forest is home to many species of moths and butterflies. These flying insects spend most of their time in the forest's canopy and understory. One square mile (2.6 km) of South America's Amazon rain forest may be home to as many as 1500 species of butterflies. There are only 750 species in all of the United States and Canada combined.

Butterflies and moths begin their lives as eggs. The eggs hatch into crawling, ravenous caterpillars. This is known as the *larva stage*. Caterpillars spend their entire lives eating leaves. The caterpillars then pass into the *pupa stage* where they spin cocoons. Although cocoons appear to be lifeless, many changes are occurring inside. When the cocoons open, beautiful butterflies or magnificent moths emerge. This process is called *metamorphosis*.

Activity

Use the following story starters to develop your creative writing. Then complete the projects on pages 52–55.

1. When I was just a little caterpillar, I really liked it when...

2. When I leave this cocoon, I'm going to...

3. I am a morpho butterfly, the largest and most beautiful butterfly in the jungle. I can...

4. Late one night, while I was out hunting with Murray Moth...

5. All the butterflies were attending the Butterfly Ball. Suddenly...

6. Megan and Mortimer Moth were heading straight for the bright light. Little did they know...

Challenges:

- Write your own story starters and exchange with a classmate.

- Write your story in a storybook format. Add illustrations. Share your butterfly story with a younger student.

- Create a poster showing the process of metamorphosis. Illustrate and label each stage in the butterfly's life.

Beautiful Butterflies

(A Stained Glass Creation)

Materials:

- butterfly pattern on page 53
- black construction paper, 12" x 18" (30 x 46 cm)
- old crayons
- plastic knife
- pencil sharpener
- wax paper
- newspaper (plenty to protect iron and work area)
- glue
- an iron
- yarn
- scissors

Directions:

1. Cut out the butterfly pattern on all solid lines. Take a sheet of 12" x 18" (30 cm x 46 cm) black construction paper and fold in half, putting the short ends together. Trace the butterfly pattern onto the construction paper. Cut out the double paper so that you end up with two identical butterflies.

2. Using either the plastic knife or pencil sharpener, shave crayon bits onto a sheet of wax paper approximately 10 inches (25 cm) long.

3. Cover the shavings with another piece of wax paper the same size.

4. Carefully place wax paper "sandwich" onto a thick layer of newspaper and cover with another two sheets of newspapers.

5. Using an iron (set on the coolest setting), iron the wax paper together so that the shavings melt inside the wax paper.

6. Glue one butterfly cutout to the crayoned wax paper. Trim the excess wax paper.

7. Place the second butterfly directly on top of the first. Glue butterflies together so the wax paper is sandwiched between both halves.

8. Attach a piece of yarn to hang up your beautiful butterfly.

Beautiful Butterflies *(cont.)*

Butterfly Pattern

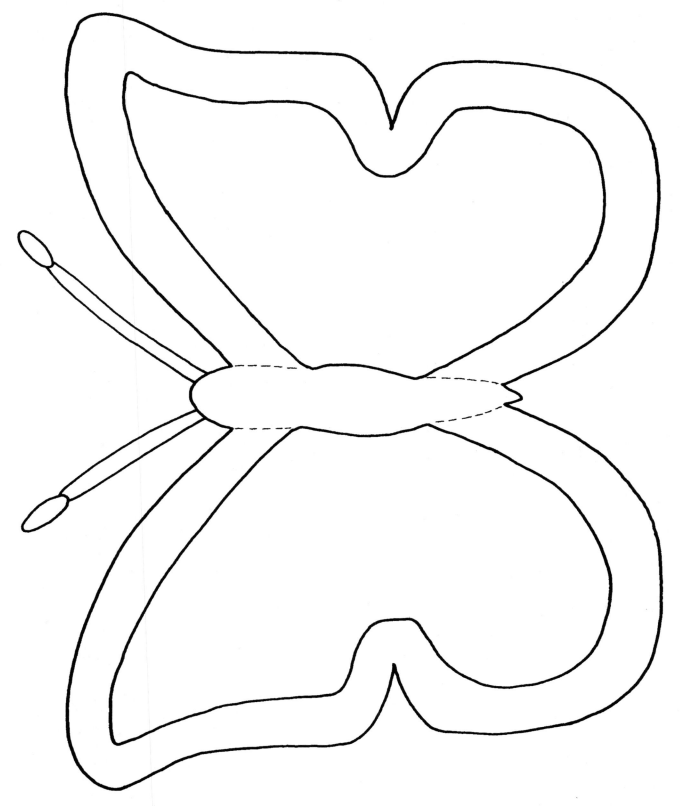

Morpho Mania

With brilliant, shimmering blue wings, the morpho butterfly spends much of its time fluttering in the upper canopy of the South American rain forest. Its iridescent blue color helps it to attract mates but also makes it noticeable to predators in the sunlight.

These quick, agile flyers are difficult to catch. They are able to make themselves seem to disappear when they close their wings or enter shady areas. The adult morpho feeds on nectar and fermenting fruit and assists in flower pollination.

Materials:

- pencils
- light-colored construction paper, 12" x 18" (30 x 46 cm)
- Morpho Mania pattern, page 55
- scissors

Directions:

1. Brainstorm words that describe butterflies.
2. Cut out the Morpho Mania butterfly pattern.
3. Fold a 12" x 18" (30 x 46 cm) piece of light-colored construction paper in half so that the short ends meet.
4. Match the dotted line of the pattern to the fold and trace the pattern onto construction paper.
5. Cut out the construction paper butterfly.
6. On the left wing of the butterfly pattern, write an adverb beginning with each letter in the word "butterfly."
7. On the right wing, write an adjective beginning with each letter in the word "butterfly."
8. When each list is complete, put the adverbs and adjectives together on the construction paper butterfly to form descriptive phrases creating a poem.

Sample:

B—beautiful blue
U—uniquely unreal
T—tirelessly traveling
T—tenderly touching
E—extremely exotic
R—radiantly real
F—flowingly funny
L—lusciously live
Y—youthfully young

Morpho Mania *(cont.)*

Butterfly Pattern

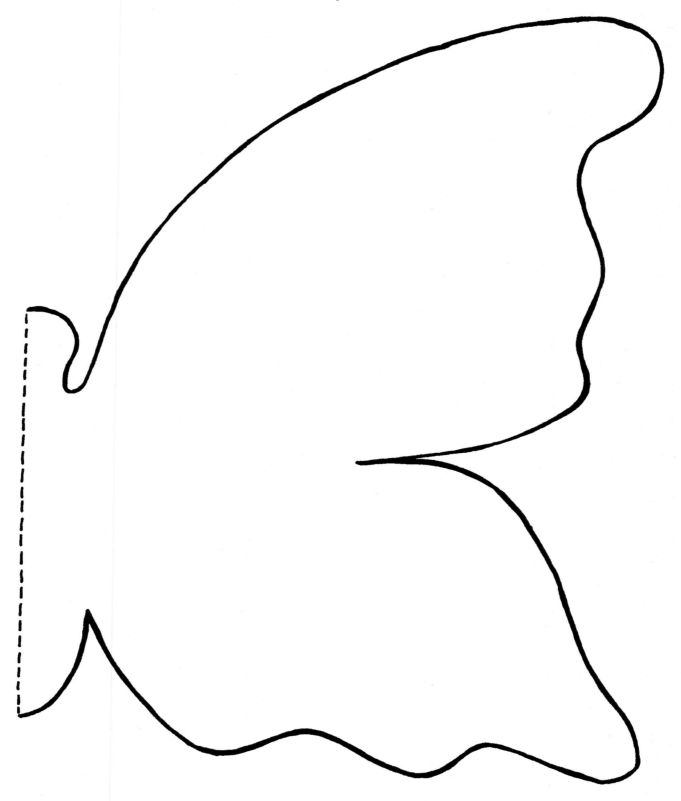

Animal Brain Strain

This problem has only one solution. To fill in the chart, mark an "X" in each square which is eliminated by a clue. When there is only one blank square left in a row or column within a category, put a happy face in that square.

Activity

A sloth, a spider monkey, a tree frog, and a toucan are named Fred, Harvey, Melissa, and Jana. Read the clues below to find each animal's name.

Clues:

1. Melissa is a different color than both the spider monkey and Jana.
2. The frog is younger than Fred.
3. Harvey is the oldest and is a good friend of the spider monkey.
4. Harvey and the toucan share the same tree.
5. Jana is not an amphibian.

Animal Brain Strain Chart

	Fred	Harvey	Melissa	Jana
Tree Frog				
Spider Monkey				
Sloth				
Toucan				

Let's Get Batty

Bats are found all over the world. They primarily live in trees and caves and flourish in the tropical rain forests. There are many species of bats, and they are all nocturnal (sleep during the day and hunt at night). We primarily think of bats as insect eaters; however, the rain forest bats eat fruit, flowers, birds, and fish, and some even eat blood.

The saying "blind as a bat" is not true since many bats have excellent vision. Bats use a unique system called *echolocation* to find their way around. They achieve this by sending out a high-pitched noise that bounces off objects and returns as an echo to the bat's ears. This echo allows the bat to judge distance, location, and size of objects.

Bats play an important role in the ecological balance of the rain forest. Insect-eating bats are valuable in controlling the multitudes of night-flying insects. Many of these insects damage crops. Some insect-eating bats are capable of consuming over six hundred insects per hour.

Nectar-eating bats are vital to seed dispersal and pollination in the tropical rain forest. These bats have physically adapted to become more efficient in the collection of nectar. Their pointed faces, long, hairy tongues, and long noses are ideally shaped for nectar gathering. Cross pollination occurs as the bat's fur collects pollen while he dines on nectar. The pollen is transferred as the bat feeds on the next blossom.

Flying foxes and other fruit-eating bats are the tropical rain forest seed-dispersers. To avoid predators, these bats munch on their fruit as they fly. During flight they eliminate large quantities of undigested seeds, thus regenerating the rain forest with the plants that grow from these seeds. It has been proven that these bats are responsible for ninety-five percent of all seeds that fall on deforested land.

The following rain forest products are dependent upon bats for seed dispersal and therefore their survival: balsa wood, kapok fiber and oil, carob, cashews, cloves, peaches, papaya, palm hearts, dates, figs, mangoes, avocados, and bananas.

Challenges:

1. Bat Awareness—Create a slogan, poster, song, rap, or bumper sticker to educate the public about the importance of bats and the need to conserve them. Keep your message simple and "catchy."

2. Bats have a very negative image from the legends surrounding the vampire bat. After doing some research, create a chart which compares the facts about bats to the fiction which you have heard.

Let's Get Batty *(cont.)*

Activity

Make your own "Batty Mobile" using the materials and directions below. When you are finished, display your mobile in the classroom.

Materials:

- unlined white paper
- construction paper (any color)
- crayons or markers
- string
- straws or twigs

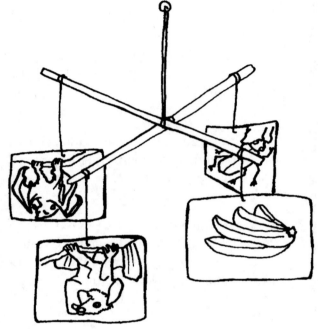

Directions:

1. On an approximately 5" x 5" (13 cm x 13 cm) square of unlined white paper, draw and color a picture of a rain forest fruit bat.

2. On a separate piece of the same size paper, draw the fruit that this bat eats.

3. Paste the picture of the fruit bat onto the front of a 6" x 6" (15 cm x 15 cm) square of colored construction paper.

4. Paste the picture of the fruit onto the back of the same piece of construction paper that the bat is on.

5. Continue this process for a nectar-eating bat, flying fox bat, and an insect-eating bat.

6. Punch a hole in the top of each completed square of construction paper.

7. Cut four pieces of string approximately 12" (30 cm) long and tie each piece of string to a finished bat square.

8. To hang your batty mobile, form an "X" with either 2 straws or 2 twigs and tie at the center where they cross.

9. Attach finished squares to either the straws or the twigs by tying the unattached end of the string to the ends of the straws (twigs).

10. Hang your batty mobile from the ceiling, using another piece of string attached to the center of the "X" on the mobile.

Groovy Grasshoppers

A grasshopper is a six-legged insect which lives, among other places, in rain forests. Its two front pairs of legs are short and thin while the hind pair is long, wider, and very powerful. The grasshopper uses only its hind legs for jumping.

Activity

A grasshopper can jump twenty times its own length. It is able to land without killing itself because of its light weight and use of wings. You can make a grasshopper jump by touching its belly.

Follow the diagrams step by step to create an original grasshopper.

1.
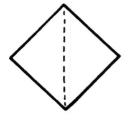
Start with a square piece of paper. Fold down the middle to make a triangle.

2.

Fold the two bottom corners up to meet at the top point.

3.
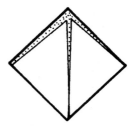
The paper should now be diamond shaped.

4.
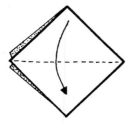
Turn the diamond over and fold it in half.

5.
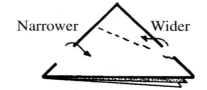
Narrower   Wider

Fold the two flaps up unevenly so that the points are above the top

6.

Draw a face and legs on your grasshopper.

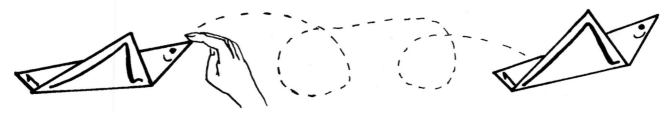

To make your grasshopper jump, quickly tap its nose.

Challenge: A real grasshopper can jump twenty times its own length. Measure the length of your grasshopper and multiply it by twenty. Then hold a contest to see whose grasshopper can jump the closest to this distance.

Fit for a Frog

The tropical rain forests have an incredible diversity of frogs and toads, known as anurans. Some of the most colorful rain forest frogs are poison-dart frogs found in Costa Rica and parts of Ecuador and Colombia. Some of these species face extinction because their forest homes are being destroyed. Certain species of these poison-dart frogs have glands in their skin which produce very toxic poisons. The native people use these poisons to coat their darts or arrows for hunting.

Frogs are cold-blooded amphibians that live part of the time in water and part of the time on land. They can not generate their own body heat. Instead, they soak up heat and sun from the air. They can grow up to 10 inches (25 cm) long. The frog's tongue is sticky, which helps it catch insects.

Frogs go through metamorphosis (changes). They hatch from jelly-like eggs. Their back legs grow first as they begin their change from tadpole (or polliwog) to adult frog. The tail then gets shorter, and the lungs and legs begin to develop. The final stage of metamorphosis is when they become adult frogs.

Activity

Let's hop to it and practice measurement in teams of three to four students. (Before this activity begins, the teacher should determine the exact amount of hops each team member will take. This will allow for adjustments for various age groups and available space.)

1. One at a time, each team member hops the determined amount of hops.

2. The total distance is measured and recorded for each student.

3. Determine which team member hopped the furthest.

4. Calculate the total distance each team hopped.

5. Calculate the average distance hopped by each team.

6. Determine which group had the highest total distance hopped.

7. Determine which group had the highest average distance hopped.

8. Add each team's total together to calculate the class total.

9. What was the average hopping distance for the whole class?

Challenge:

Research to find out how far various types of frogs are capable of jumping. Put this information on a chart or graph.

Insect Creations

Insects live nearly everywhere on earth. There are more than 800,000 kinds of insects already named by scientists. It is believed that the rain forests contain millions of types of insects, many of which are undiscovered and unclassified.

Activity

Use the following characteristics and your imagination to create an insect. Name it after the famous scientist who is first bringing it to the world's attention—you!

- All insects have three body parts—head, thorax, and abdomen.

- All insects have six jointed legs.

- The head has eyes, antennae, and a mouth that sucks or chews.

- The thorax has six legs (three on each side) and usually four wings. Some wings help an insect fly, and some wings protect. Wings are always symmetrical—one side is the same size, shape, and color as the other.

- The abdomen has ten or eleven segments. You can usually see five to eight of them.

Use the patterns below (or make some of your own) to create your insect. Trace them on construction paper, cut them out, and glue them together. Be sure your insect has three body parts and six jointed legs. Add color and details with crayon, markers, tissue paper, etc.

Monkey Bread

Rain forests are home to many species of monkeys. One of the noisiest species of monkeys is the howler monkey. Their voices can be carried for about one and a half miles through the forest. They howl each morning when they wake up as a warning to other howler groups to stay away. They howl their warning again as they settle down for the night.

They live in groups of up to 30 animals and stay together in their search for food. The howler monkey uses its tail as an extra arm or leg to wrap around branches as it swings through the trees, looking for its favorite foods, wild fruit and nuts.

Enjoy the following recipe using the monkey's favorite foods!

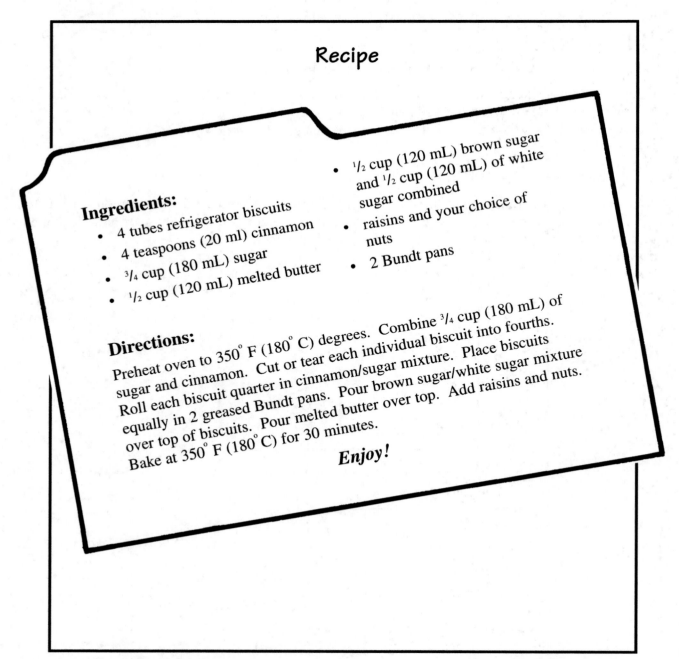

Recipe

Ingredients:

- 4 tubes refrigerator biscuits
- 4 teaspoons (20 ml) cinnamon
- ³/₄ cup (180 mL) sugar
- ¹/₂ cup (120 mL) melted butter
- ¹/₂ cup (120 mL) brown sugar and ¹/₂ cup (120 mL) of white sugar combined
- raisins and your choice of nuts
- 2 Bundt pans

Directions:

Preheat oven to 350° F (180° C) degrees. Combine ³/₄ cup (180 mL) of sugar and cinnamon. Cut or tear each individual biscuit into fourths. Roll each biscuit quarter in cinnamon/sugar mixture. Place biscuits equally in 2 greased Bundt pans. Pour brown sugar/white sugar mixture over top of biscuits. Pour melted butter over top. Add raisins and nuts. Bake at 350° F (180° C) for 30 minutes.

Enjoy!

Monkeying Around

The monkeys were in a playful mood one day, and they mixed up a list of rain forest plants and animals. Please help unscramble the following words.

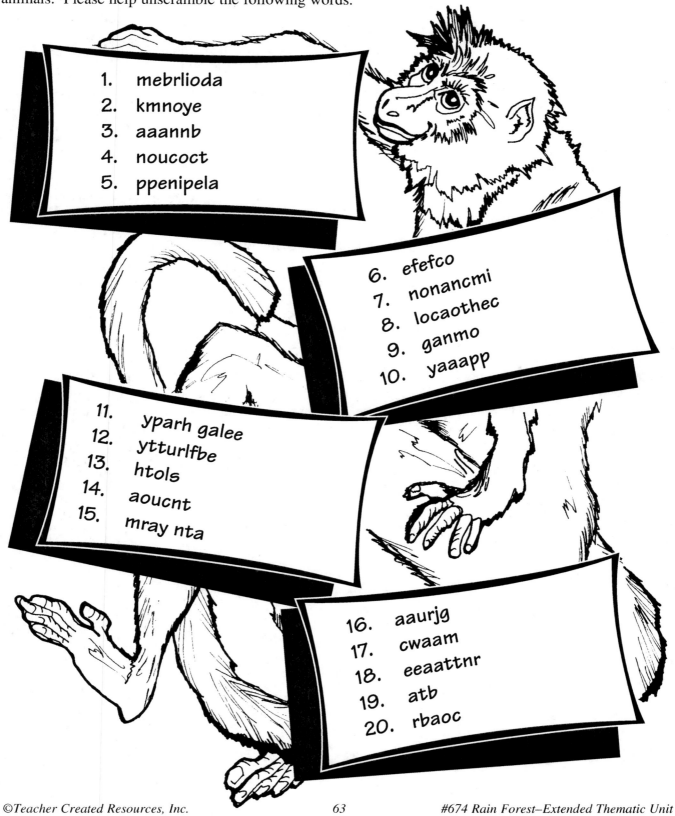

1. mebrlioda
2. kmnoye
3. aaannb
4. noucoct
5. ppenipela

6. efefco
7. nonancmi
8. locaothec
9. ganmo
10. yaaapp

11. yparh galee
12. ytturlfbe
13. htols
14. aoucnt
15. mray nta

16. aaurjg
17. cwaam
18. eeaattnr
19. atb
20. rbaoc

Life in the Tropical Rain Forest–Plants

This section focuses on the uniqueness and importance of rain forest plants. Plants that have disappeared from other parts of the world are still alive today in the rain forest.

How Important Are Plants?

- Trees produce oxygen and consume carbon dioxide. The rain forests of Amazonia produce about 40% of the world's oxygen!

- To maintain and improve resistance to pests and disease, domestic plants are crossbred with the genetic material from their wild relatives found in tropical forests.

- The plants and animals of the rain forests have been living on Earth in a remarkable ecosystem for hundreds of thousands of years. Many have not yet been discovered, named, or studied. They offer enormous and potential benefits to humankind.

Suggestions for Extending the Section

Use the Plant Illustrations (pages 71 and 72) as visual aids while teaching about rain forest plants.

Create a rain forest coloring book using the plants and animals found in the rain forest. Each student will research one rain forest plant or animal in order to create one page in the class coloring book. Each page should include some important information about the plant or animal and an illustration to color. (This book can be used as a sale item in the Rain Forest Museum, Section VIII.)

Contents of This Section

Leaf Me Alone!

Rain forest plants have evolved in some incredible ways in order to survive, from the vines that strangle trees to get sunlight to plants that produce poisons which discourage animals from eating them. Plants found in the understory, like herbs, shrubs, and small trees, have adapted to growing in the shade. Others have developed special strategies to get their fair share of the sun.

Epiphytes

An epiphyte is a plant that grows on another plant but does not harm it. The roots of many epiphytes can absorb moisture directly from the air; therefore, they are often called air plants. These epiphytes are able to obtain the sunlight they need because they grow high above the dim forest floor. Many ferns, bromeliads, mosses, and orchids are examples of epiphytes.

Epiphytes have also developed special characteristics to help them obtain needed water. Some store water inside their stems, while others send out aerial roots which absorb moisture directly from the air.

Vines

Vines have adapted a unique way to get the sunlight they need. They root in the ground, and as they grow towards the sun they climb up a convenient tree. Some climb straight up, while others twist around the tree's trunk, using hooks or tendrils to attach themselves.

Lianas are twining vines that have thick, flexible, woody stems. They wind around the trees that support them. If the supporting tree dies and decays, the lianas are left hanging from the forest canopy. Liana stems make a natural rope. The fictional movie character, Tarzan, used lianas to swing from one tree to another across the jungle.

Defensive Plants

Some rain forest plants have developed a defense system against animal predators. While some plants produce chemicals which make their leaves distasteful, other grow sharp prickles or spines as their means of defense. There are trees that produce leaves full of poison (such as caffeine, morphine, tannin, and terpene) to keep away plant eating animals. Many of these same chemicals have been found useful in the production of medicine. Other rain forest trees have developed slippery barks, making it very difficult for strangling vines to cling to them.

Natural Drug Store

Over half of the drugs that we use today were discovered in tropical rain forest plants, like quinine (used to fight malaria), curare (an anesthetic and muscle relaxant used in surgery), and cancer fighting drugs. One can only guess how many more drugs are awaiting discovery in the rain forest.

Drip Tips

Rain Forest trees have learned to protect themselves from the abundance of falling rain by developing leaves with drip tips. These leaves come to a point (tip) allowing the rainwater to roll off, thereby inhibiting the growth of fungus.

Leaf Me Alone *(cont.)*

Activity

Create a rain forest necklace using the following salt dough directions.

Materials:

- 1 ½ cups (340 g) flour
- ¾ cup (170 g) water
- wax paper
- food coloring
- mixing bowl
- ¾ cup (170 g) salt
- plastic knives
- rolling pin
- thin leather strips (sold in craft stores) or yarn

Directions:

1. Mix food coloring with the water. Add the flour and salt. (Slowly add more water if needed.)
2. Knead ingredients into a workable dough.
3. Divide dough among students.
4. Flatten salt dough on wax paper. Use a rolling pin, if desired.
5. With a plastic knife cut out a shape that resembles a rain forest leaf or plant.
6. Poke two holes through the top of your shape.
7. Allow the salt dough to dry.
8. Thread the yarn or leather strip through the two holes and tie the ends together to make a necklace.

Note: You may wish to use this activity in conjunction with the Rain Forest Museum (see Section IX). The necklaces could be sold in the Museum Gift Shop as a fund-raiser to help save the rain forest.

Mysterious Plants

Plant and animal partnerships are very important to the survival of the rain forests. These interactions may mean the difference between life or death for many species. The removal of just one species can disrupt the lives of many other species. What do you think would happen if a large portion of the rain forest were to disappear?

In order to compete for the limited resources, rain forest plants and animals have developed highly specialized techniques for survival. Pollination is the best example of plant and animal partnerships. Most of the plants in the rain forest depend upon animals for pollination.

Insects, bats, and birds are the most common pollinators of rain forest plants. Many rain forest plants and animals have developed an exclusive partnership for pollination; for example, the color, shape, or smell of a flower attracts specific animals.

Plant Facts:

❀ An orchid in Madagascar hides its nectar six inches deep in a narrow tube so that only the long-tongued hawk moth can reach it, pollinating the flower at the same time.

❀ The rafflesia plant grows on the forest floor in Asia. It produces flowers that are three feet in diameter—it is the biggest flower in the world! They have thick, warty petals, and spiky centers that smell like rotting meat, which attracts pollinating flies.

❀ The cecropia tree is home to the Azteca ants. These ants protect the tree by stinging animal intruders. In addition, they destroy any nearby plants which might intrude on the cecropia's space in the forest.

❀ Leafcutter ants chew up small pieces of leaves, stems, and flowers in their underground nests. These leaves, stems, and flowers (which they do not eat) serve as a medium for fungus to grow. The ants allow the fungus to grow by chewing the leaves, etc., and the fungus becomes food for the ants.

Activity

Draw a picture to illustrate an interdependent relationship of a plant and animal living in the tropical rain forest. Draw another illustration showing what would happen if a plant or animal species is removed.

Outrageous Orchids

Although orchids are found almost everywhere in the world, the most extraordinary ones grow in the rain forest. This tough, common flower is part of the largest family of flowering plants, called Orchidaceae. Contrary to popular belief, it is also one of the easiest plants to grow and produces the strangest and most beautiful flowers. There are approximately 20,000–30,000 different species of orchids.

Most tropical orchids are epiphytes, or air plants, that grow on trees or rocks without harming them. Orchids use the trees only for support—they are not parasites. Tropical orchids have aerial roots which are important because they allow the orchid to collect nutrients from the tiny particles of organic matter in rainwater. They also secure the orchid to its host.

Some orchids are even edible! The pod of the vanilla bean orchid is used to give a vanilla flavor to some foods and beverages. In fact, the word "vanilla" means "little pod" in reference to the orchid pod from which it comes. Other orchids are also often used in creating cold medicines or for flavoring various foods and drinks.

The seeds of an orchid are so tiny that a million of them can be produced by a single plant. An orchid seed is sometimes carried by the wind until it attaches itself to the lichen on a tree. During tropical rainstorms the seed swells, beginning an incredible partnership. Fungus spores enter the swelling orchid seed and eventually encase it in a jelly-like material which helps the orchid germinate. The orchid is not harmed by the fungus. The fungus needs the orchid to produce food for it since fungi do not produce their own food. When both partners mutually benefit from a relationship, it is called *symbiosis.*

Another way in which an orchid spreads its seeds is by flying animals. Some orchids have adapted themselves so that animals will be more likely to help them pollinate. Creatures such as insects and birds carry the seeds to different areas of the rain forest where the seeds are dropped. The seeds eventually grow, and these new orchids sometimes need to adapt themselves to their new surroundings. The adaptations caused by pollination through flying animals partially accounts for the great diversity in the Orchidaceae family.

Outrageous Orchids *(cont.)*

Read the following stories describing relationships. If they are describing a symbiotic relationship, put an S on the line. If they are not symbiotic, put an NS on the line.

Remember, a symbiotic relationship means that the association of two different organisms creates benefits for each individual organism.

1. _____ Richard, the bank manager, has stolen a great deal of money from the bank. Due to a loss of funds the bank is forced to close.

2. _____ Charlie, the cocker spaniel, lives with his owner, Harvey Fritzmeyer. Harvey feeds and cares for Charlie. Charlie guards the house and gives Harvey lots of affection.

3. _____ Irma the clown fish feeds on the leftovers from the poisonous sea anemone. Irma's feeding habits keep the sea anemone clean.

4. _____ Lamprey eels feed off the blood of other fish by attaching themselves to the fish. The fish grows weaker while the lamprey eel becomes stronger.

5. _____ Mrs. Miller, the teacher, helps her students with a difficult math concept. The students all earn "A's" on their exams. Mrs. Miller is happy.

6. _____ Thomas Jefferson High School and Woodrow Wilson High School both have losing football teams. They decide to put their best players together to form one team. This new team wins the state championship. Both schools take home a trophy.

7. _____ Plants produce oxygen which humans need to breathe. Humans exhale carbon dioxide which plants need for photosynthesis.

8. _____ A lumberjack cuts down all of the trees in a small forest and does not replant. The lumber is sold to be processed into paper products.

Bountiful Bromeliads

Bromeliads are a family of plants that include the pineapple. Many bromeliads grow on other plants. They collect rainwater in their cup-like centers and have stiff, spiky leaves. The hairs on the leaves absorb water so it can be used by the plant. A large bromeliad can hold over one gallon (3.8 l) of water and serve as home for insects and small water animals.

Activity

Test your "Pineapple Power." Use the information below to grow your own pineapple.

Materials:

- 1 fresh pineapple (make sure top is fresh and green)
- 1 medium flower pot
- potting soil
- pebbles
- 1 large plastic bag

Directions:

1. Cut off the leafy top of the pineapple, leaving about one-third of the fruit attached. Allow the top to dry overnight.

2. The next day, scrape away any fruit that is still soft, making sure not to scrape the center core of the pineapple.

3. Place a layer of the pebbles on the bottom of the pot.

4. Fill the pot about three-quarters full with moist potting soil.

5. Place the cut pineapple top into the soil.

6. Cover the top of the pineapple and pot with the large plastic bag and place it in a warm, sunny place.

7. When new leaves begin to appear in the center, remove the bag.

8. Watch your pineapple plant grow into a bountiful bromeliad. (If you are lucky, eventually a new baby pineapple may appear.)

Plant Illustrations

Fern

Pineapple

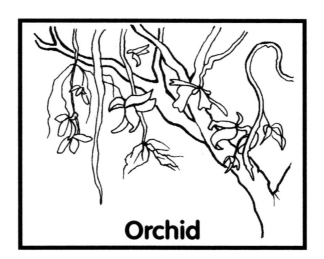

Orchid

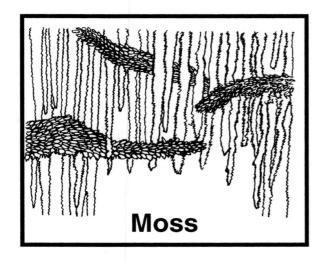

Moss

Liana Vines

Plant Illustrations *(cont.)*

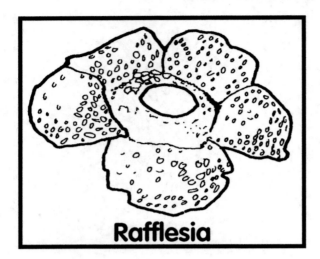

Rafflesia

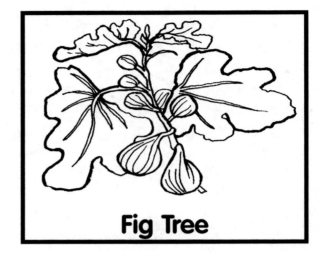

Fig Tree

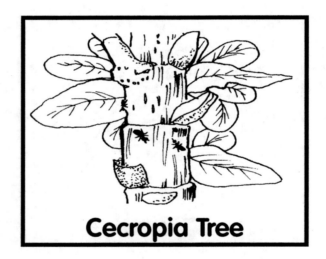

Cecropia Tree

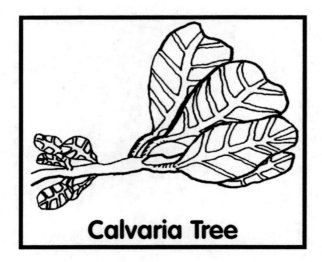

Calvaria Tree

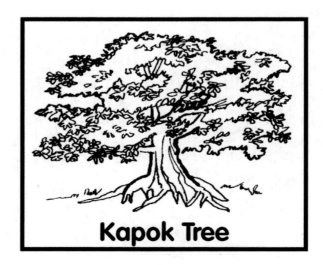

Kapok Tree

To Tree or Not to Tree

Miguel and his family are very poor and have only a few mature trees left on their land. There are no other trees for miles around. It is a record-breaking cold winter, they have used up all of their firewood, and the winter has barely begun. They must decide how they will keep warm through the rest of the winter and how they will get more fuel for cooking (they cook on a wood burning stove). They consider chopping down some or all of their trees.

Activity

- What should Miguel and his family do? In cooperative groups, discuss and debate what would happen if they decide to cut down all of the trees.

- What would happen if they cut down all the trees for firewood?

- What would happen to the animals that call these trees their home?

- What would happen during the hot summer months?

- What would happen next winter when they need more firewood?

- What would happen next winter when they need to keep warm?

  Think about long-term and short-term effects of cutting down all of the trees.

- What would be the long-term effects of this action?

- Think globally. What would happen if all the people in similar situations cut down all the trees on their properties?

- How can you relate this situation to what is happening to our rain forests today?

- What would you do to ensure that there would be trees left on earth for the future?

Challenge:

Write a letter to your senator, telling him or her why you think that it is important to save the rain forest. Ask him or her to do whatever is possible to help save the world's disappearing rain forests. Send your letters to:

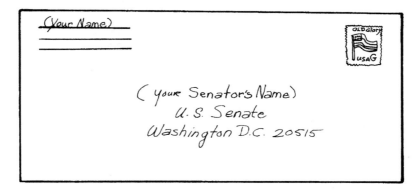

Pull-Out Paper Tree

In some parts of the tropics, rainfall is year round and the weather is always hot. These conditions produce broad-leaved trees that can grow at an extraordinary rate. Some grow as much as fifteen feet (five meters) a year. The broad leaves help to absorb the sunlight in the dim understory of the jungle.

Activity

Create a newspaper tree. When you are done, display your trees as suggested at the bottom of this page.

Materials:

- newspaper
- scissor
- ruler
- green tempera paint
- tape
- coffee can

Directions:

1. Take two sheets of newspaper. Starting with the shorter side, roll newspaper into a tube with a diameter of approximately 2 inches (5 cm). Place a piece of tape at the middle and the bottom of the tube.

2. Make four cuts each about 6 inches (15 cm) long into the top of the tube.

3. Reach inside and gently pull the insides up and out.

4. Paint the finished paper tree.

5. Decorate your tree with paper birds, or butterflies, or a tree frog.

6. "Plant" your tree in the coffee can, using crumpled newspaper to secure it.

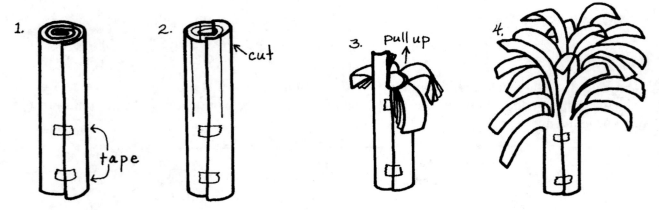

Suggested Uses:

1. Use completed paper trees as plants and small bushes on the forest floor of the Rain Forest Museum (see Section VIII).

2. Construct additional paper trees in various sizes to represent plants, large bushes, trees, etc., for the understory layers.

Reach for the Sky

An elusive and extraordinarily mysterious world exists in the tropical treetops. Scientists have just begun to explore this unique and luxurious environment. Little is known about life in this skyscraper habitat because of its inaccessibility. In order to truly understand how plants and animals live, it is necessary for them to be studied in their natural habitat.

The conditions in the treetops contrast vastly from those on the forest floor. High up in the treetops the sun and wind are much stronger, and the rainfall is heavier. When an animal's natural habitat is intruded upon in any way, it can become frightened. It takes time for the animals to adjust to anything unfamiliar.

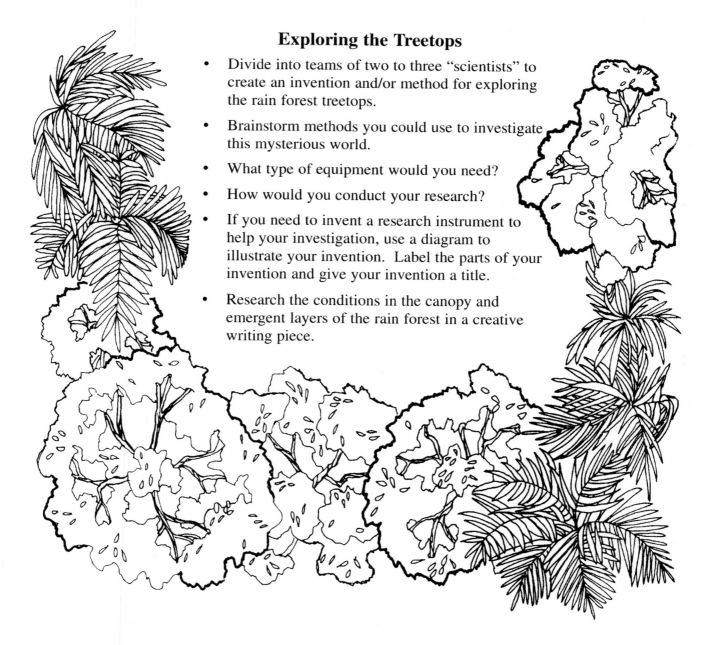

Exploring the Treetops

- Divide into teams of two to three "scientists" to create an invention and/or method for exploring the rain forest treetops.

- Brainstorm methods you could use to investigate this mysterious world.

- What type of equipment would you need?

- How would you conduct your research?

- If you need to invent a research instrument to help your investigation, use a diagram to illustrate your invention. Label the parts of your invention and give your invention a title.

- Research the conditions in the canopy and emergent layers of the rain forest in a creative writing piece.

Plant Brain Strain

This problem has only one solution. To fill in the chart, mark an "X" in each square which is eliminated by a clue. When there is only one blank square left in a row or column within a category, put a happy face in that square.

Activity

The favorite rain forest trees and plants of David, Adam, Bianca, and Chelsey are bromeliads, orchids, ferns, and kapok trees. Read the clues below to find each person's favorite rain forest tree or plant.

Clues:

1. No person's name has the same number of letters as his or her favorite rain forest tree or plant.

2. David and the boy who likes orchids are from different tribes.

3. The kapok tree is the favorite of one of the girls.

4. Chelsey's favorite plant is a member of the pineapple family.

Chart
Plant Brain Strain

	David	Adam	Bianca	Chelsey
Bromeliad				
Orchid				
Fern				
Kapok Tree				

Designer Plant

Through a process called *photosynthesis*, green plants use sunlight to produce food. Trees and plants which are found in the canopy and emergent layers live in a sunnier and drier atmosphere than those found in the understory or forest floor. Plants found in the understory have adapted to less sunlight by developing broad flat leaves. Other plants absorb their food and nutrition directly from other plants. Therefore, they are not dependent on sunlight to survive.

Plants need nutrients to grow, and they receive these nutrients in a variety of ways. Many absorb them through their root systems; however, there are not many nutrients in tropical rain forest soil (they all wash away with the rain). Therefore, plants store most of the nutrients they need in their leaves and stems. Nutrients can also be found in a thin layer of decaying vegetation found on the forest floor. Epiphytes (ferns, bromeliads, orchids, etc.) trap falling bits of vegetation and water in their basket-like shapes.

Understory leaves stay wet, encouraging lichens, molds, and fungi to grow. Constantly wet leaves encourage this growth, which prevents the plants from getting their needed sunlight. To reduce this problem, many plants have drip tips (smooth leaves with points at the end where the water can drip off easily). Other plants have smooth, waxy leaves which help rid them of excess water.

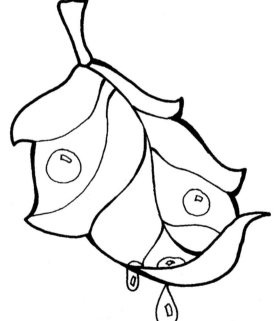

Due to the enormous height of many rain forest trees (65 feet/20 meters or taller), scientists believe that they have adapted a specialized root system. Special support-like buttress roots or stick-like stilt roots help keep the tree from being blown over by spreading the tree's ponderous weight.

Plants discourage leaf-eating insects and animals in unique ways. Some produce poisonous or foul tasting chemicals. Some have spines on their leaves or thorns on their stems, and some have developed symbiotic relationships with insects.

There are other ways to absorb water besides a plant's root system. An orchid's aerial roots can absorb moisture directly from the air around them. Bromeliad leaves grow in a basket-like shape where water can collect like a miniature pond. These miniature ponds provide an environment for a multitude of rain forest life.

Rain forest plants and trees depend upon animals, such as the fruit bat, for pollination. The wind also carries seeds for pollination.

Designer Plant *(cont.)*

Design and draw an original plant or tree that can survive in a tropical rain forest environment. As you create, consider the questions below. Label all of the parts. Then, on a separate piece of paper, answer the questions about your plant.

1. In which layer of the rain forest does your plant grow?

2. Tell about its leaves and root system.

3. How is it pollinated?

4. How does your plant receive its nutrients and water?

5. How does your plant get the sunlight it needs?

6. How does your plant defend itself from being eaten?

7. How does your plant defend itself against molds?

Rain Forest Brain Stretchers

Closely follow the directions below to write five sentences about the rain forest.

1. In the first sentence, use the word *canopy* as the sixth word.

    _____

    _____

2. In the second sentence, write the word *epiphyte* two times.

    _____

    _____

3. In the third sentence, put the word *equator* in the last position.

    _____

    _____

4. In the fourth sentence, use the word *extinct* anywhere.

    _____

    _____

5. In the fifth sentence, use the word *sloth* as the fourth word.

    _____

    _____

Challenge:

Choose one of these sentences as a topic sentence and write a paragraph about it. You may add an illustration.

Rain Forest Story Starters

The waters of the Amazon are rising rapidly...

Thrashing your way through the jungle with a machete, you suddenly feel something land on the back of your neck...

Going down the crocodile–infested Amazon, your boat hits a hidden sandbar and quickly begins to sink...

Walking through the jungle, you come across a camp of poachers. You know this is a protected area. You...

A harpy eagle swoops down and steals the last of your food rations...

After many years of jungle research for new medicines, a native introduces you to a special plant. It can...

You are on a food gathering expedition in the jungle. You suddenly realize you are separated from the others...

You awake to a strange howling sound. Big yellow eyes are staring back at you in the dark...

You have been reduced to the size of an ant. You climb on the wings of a Morpho butterfly and...

You are walking through the rain forest when you hear a crashing noise behind you. You turn around and see...

Camping in the jungle, your expedition is attacked by a tribe of cannibals...

Your plane crashes in the jungle...

Pick a Plant

Circle the following words in the word search.

Amaryllis	Cannonball Tree	Frangiplant	Philodendron
Anthurium	Cassava	Heliconia	Piper
Banana	Cecropia	Hibiscus	Poinciana
Bird's Nest Fungus	Ceiba	Liana	Sensitive Plant
Blood Flower	Coconut Palm	Mahogany	Strangler
Bougainvillea	Coffee	Mango	Sugarcane
Breadfruit	Cordia	Monstera	Tea
Bromeliad	Cup Fungus	Orchid	Tropical Tree
Buttressed Roots	Drip Tips	Parasol Fungus	Yellow Poui
Cacao	Earth Ball Fungus	Passion Flower	

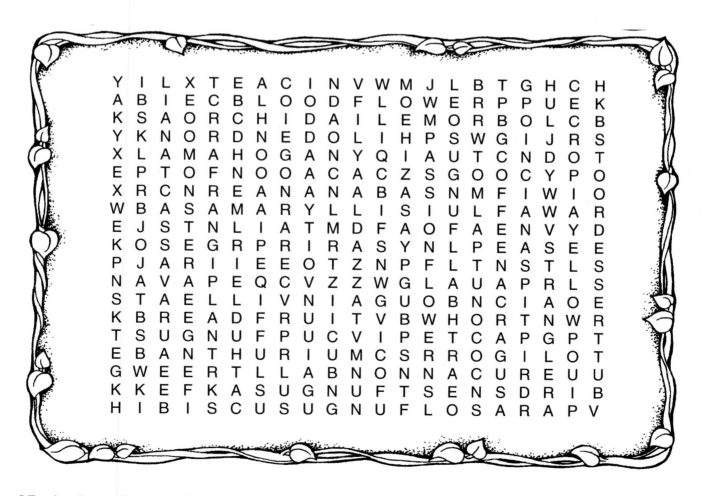

Tropical Tongue Twisters

Tongue twisters are phrases that are difficult to repeat quickly. See how quickly you can say the following tongue twisters clearly and correctly.

- She sells sea shells by the seashore, she sells seashells by the seashore,...
- Three thin tree twigs, three thin tree twigs, three thin tree twigs,...
- Silver thistles, silver thistles, silver thistles,...
- Big brown baboon, big brown baboon, big brown baboon,...
- Six sick sloths, six sick sloths, six sick sloths,...
- Red feather, yellow leather, red feather, yellow leather,...

Activity

Now, make up at least five of your own tongue twisters. Try to keep a rain forest theme.

_____

_____

_____

_____

_____

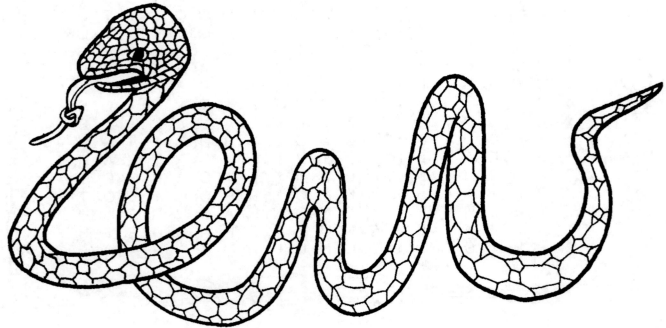

People and Products of the Rain Forest

This section focuses on some of the ways people make a living in the rain forest and the products of the rain forest that enrich our lives.

Spice of Life...and More

Whether or not we realize it, we encounter many products of the rain forest in our daily lives. In fact, it would be extremely difficult for anyone to *not* encounter a rain forest product on any given day. Fruits, nuts, flavor extracts, perfumes, medicines, and wood are just a few of the rain forest's gifts to us.

Suggestions for Extending the Section

- Have students research some of the rain forest products found in their homes.

- What plant does each product come from? From which tropical rain forests did each plant originally come? Are any of these plants now found growing outside the rain forests?

- Hang a large wall map of the world on a bulletin board. Place rain forest products or pictures of them around the map. Using colored string, connect each product to its country of origin.

- Make a collage of rain forest products found in homes today.

- Paint a mural of commonly found rain forest products.

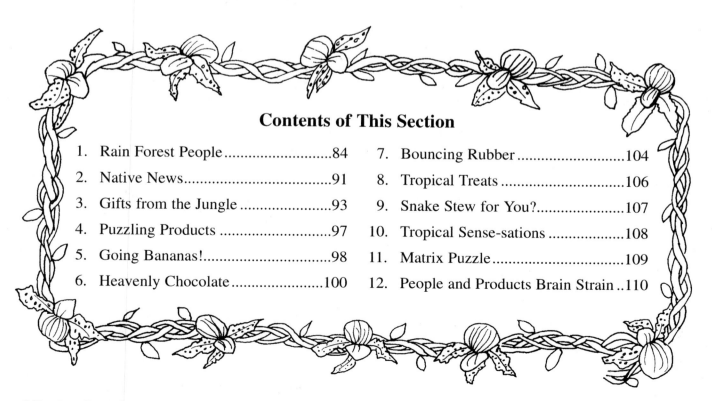

Contents of This Section

Rain Forest People

The tropical rain forest contains not only a multitude of animals and plants, but people as well. Today, there are still hundreds of rain forest cultures that continue to live a lifestyle much like that of their ancestors.

These rain forest people live in harmony with their environment as the forest plays an integral part in their daily lives. The rain forest provides them with all of their necessities; in return, they honor and respect it as is evidenced in their rituals.

While Western societies may look upon these rain forest cultures as primitive, in many ways they are far more knowledgeable and advanced than we are about the ability to function in their natural habitats. They know when certain fruits will ripen, when it is time for planting, and they work in harmony with the forest's natural cycles.

The indigenous people of the rain forest know more about the plants and animals of the rain forests than even the most educated scientists. In the Amazon Basin, the indigenous people use over two thousand different plants as pharmaceuticals.

Modern ethnobotanists are furiously studying all they can about rain forest cultures and their use of the forest to treat their illnesses—before it is too late! Ethnobotany is the study of how indigenous people use local plants.

Rain forest cultures are quickly disappearing, and as they disappear, so does the opportunity for us to learn more about our world.

Many indigenous cultures have faced destruction through contact with the outside world. Rain forest people have not yet built up immunities to many diseases. Occupants of entire jungle villages have fallen ill and died from exposure to common diseases, some as ordinary as the flu.

Another threat to the lifestyle of the rain forest people is the pressure to assimilate into other cultures. Clothing, cooking, pots, guns, and toys are being introduced as the modern world invades deeper and deeper into the forest.

The new generation is less interested in the important lessons taught by their elders. Many are choosing to leave their cultures behind in their quest to join modern society.

Rain Forest People *(cont.)*

Pygmies of the Congo

Deep in the jungle of the Ituri Forest in the Congo live the Mbuti (mm-BOO-tee) Pygmies. These nomads, who hunt and gather their food to survive, live much as their ancestors did thousands of years ago. The Mbutis identify the rain forest as the provider of life and of all beneficial things, including food, shelter, and clothing. Additionally, they view the forest as their protector from non-forest people and all harmful things.

The Mbuti Pygmies take full advantage of whatever the forest has to offer. They sometimes hunt large game, such as elephants, okapis, and buffalo, but they mostly hunt smaller animals like monkeys and birds. The women provide most of the food the Pygmies eat, either by collecting it from the forest or working for it in the villages.

The Mbuti use bows and arrows or nets for hunting. In some Mbuti groups, hunting is a cooperative effort undertaken only by the men and boys. In other groups of Mbuti Pygmies, men, women, and children all participate.

Honey season is an integral part of Mbuti culture and one they look forward to each year. During the brief season, they consume an enormous amount of honey which accounts for much of their calorie intake during the year.

The Pygmies have two features that make them quite unique, their characteristic reddish-brown skin and their small stature. Pygmies grow to be only four to four and a half feet (1.2 to 1.4 m) tall.

The Pygmies live in groups comprised of several families. In general, it is the men that hunt and collect honey while the women fish, collect wood and water, gather berries, build huts, and prepare food. Pygmy women are also the primary caretakers of the children. The children develop adult survival skills through play. Boys begin to hunt with the male elders at about age nine. Girls are trained for their chores from age three.

The Mbuti Pygmies are beautiful in their simplicity. They are not burdened with too many possessions. The forest provides them with what they need to survive. They do not negatively impact the forest because they are few in number and do not stay in one place for long periods of time. This allows the forest to replenish itself.

Rain Forest People *(cont.)*

Wayana Indians

Living in scattered communities on the northern coast of South America are the Wayanas. This group of less than one thousand Indians has survived for centuries in the remote rain forest of the Amazon region. Their settlements are so deep within the rain forest that they seldom see any sunlight. Canoes provide their only means of transportation along the Maroni and Itany Rivers.

The Wayanas once numbered over three thousand. It is believed they migrated to Guiana from northern Brazil. By 1950, due to exposure to measles and tuberculosis, there were fewer than 500 Wayanas left. Thanks to a medical program established by the French government in 1961, their numbers are increasing. Additionally, tourism was restricted in their area to reduce any future threat of epidemic diseases.

The Wayanas are a resourceful people who are expert in finding and collecting rain forest edibles. Iguana eggs are found by poking a stick into the river's sandy beaches. Smoked iguana meat produces a rich flavor contrasted to the sweet wild nuts and berries. Wild honey is gathered fresh from the comb, and crunchy, large ants are eaten alive. However, the Wayana's favorite treat is fat, juicy grubs!

Each family resides in its own home, which is raised high above the ground to protect it from rats and crawling insects. The furnishings are sparse and consist of hammocks made from webbed cotton. The hammocks are hung inside the houses at night and underneath, where it is shady, during the day.

Survival skills are taught to young children through play. Domestic chores are shared. Women traditionally prepare the manioc root to make food and drink. They also spin cotton which they weave into hammocks. The men usually construct the baskets and other straw goods. Authority and child care is shared.

An interesting and unique Wayana custom is the "ant test" known as marake. Its purpose is to prepare young men and women for physical hardship. Marake begins with dancing, storytelling, and drinking kasili, a mild fermented brew made from manioc root. Then a wicker frame, holding up to a hundred stinging ants, is applied to all parts of the child's body. The child proves to be a true Wayana by remaining still and silent.

The simplicity of the Wayana way of life is being tested by the increasing pressures form the outside world. Alcoholism has become a serious family problem. How long the Wayana culture can withstand the infiltration of outside influences remains unknown. Suicide among teenagers, previously unknown to these people, is a sign of the changing times.

Rain Forest People *(cont.)*

The Penan of Borneo

Before deforestation, almost the entire island of Borneo, in Southeast Asia, was rain forest. In the northern part of the vast and lush Sarawak rain forest, a tribe called the Penan flourished for over 40,000 years.

The total survival of the Penan depends upon hunting game and gathering fruits and nuts. Their entire diet was provided directly from nature. This has become increasingly more difficult due to the destruction of the rain forest. Food for the Penan is far more scarce than it once was.

Borneo

To hunt, the Penan use a blowpipe that stands taller than they do. They catch and eat wild boar (their staple meat), monkeys, deer, and hornbills. The blowpipe is loaded with a dart dipped in poison that is derived from tree sap. The poison is forcefully blown through the pipe towards the unsuspecting prey. When used for fishing, the end of the blowpipe is fitted with a spear.

Being nomadic people, the concept of land ownership is totally foreign to them. Like so many other rain forest people, they move freely around the rain forest as they hunt game and gather foods and natural medicines. That is, they did until the logging companies arrived!

Malaysian and foreign lumber companies, with government approval, have cut down trees in the forest. The Penan were forced to live in villages of 800 people or more. This was a major adjustment for people used to living in smaller family groups of only 20 to 30. No longer can they freely wander through the beautiful forest. Instead, in these new villages, they suffer from malnutrition and diseases they never before faced.

Logging has driven away the animals and, consequently, disrupted the hunting and fishing of the Penan. Furthermore, without trees, there is nothing to prevent the soil from flowing into the rivers during heavy rains. The rivers, therefore, have become saturated with silt, making fishing difficult.

The Penan, being a peaceful tribe, attempted to protect their way of life by erecting a blockade across the logging road at Long Ajeng. After nine months of resistance, the Malaysian government's response was to send in 1,000 riot police to force the Penan to remove the blockade. Many Penan were arrested. The logging companies were given free rein to reenter the land of the Penan without regard for the survival of the people.

Once 10,000 strong, the Penan, now only a few thousand, face an uncertain future.

Rain Forest People *(cont.)*

The People of the Amazon

More rain forest land is destroyed in Brazil than in any other country of the world. Since Brazil's rain forests were so huge, it still has more rain forest land remaining than any other country. About one-third of the world's rain forest acreage is in Brazil.

Sadly, about two percent of Brazil's remaining rain forests are cut or burned each year. If this present rate of destruction continues, in 50 years all of Brazil's rain forests will be gone.

In 1975, the Brazilian government opened an unpaved two-lane road through their rain forests. It was hoped that this Transamazon Highway would give millions of poor people in Brazil a place to live and allow companies to take advantage of the natural resources of the Amazon basin.

Brazil

The road has helped Brazilian economy, but has been disastrous for the rain forest. The road allowed farmers and ranchers to remove trees to create fields and pastures. Miners looking for gold have also arrived. The gold mining activities pollute the many rivers of the Amazon region with highly toxic metals and deplete the rain forest and pollute the air by burning enormous amounts of wood.

In 1987, gold miners brought disease to the Yanomani natives. Within three years, 15% of the population had died of tuberculosis, malaria, mumps, flu, or the common cold. Fishing in the Yanomani's rivers has been ruined by the mercury used to extract gold. The mercury now contaminates their waters, their lands, and even the people themselves.

Of the sixteen million people living in the Brazilian Amazon, only 200,000 are indigenous. Mining roads, logging, and ranching are eroding the rain forest people's very existence. The Urueu-Wau-Wau of Rondonia and the Waimiri-Atroari of the central Brazilian Amazon remain with only a few hundred people today, compared with thousands of natives in the 1970s. A project called Calha Norte, designed to bring more development into the remote jungle, is largely responsible.

Similar catastrophes for indigenous tribes are occurring in rain forests everywhere. In Chile, the Mapuche Indians face economic, health, and human rights problems. In Panama, the Guaymis suffer from land takeovers by Panamanian cattle ranchers. In Ecuador, it is road and oil pipeline construction threatening the peaceful way of life of the Waorani. This same sad story is being retold again and again in the tropical rain forests around the world.

Rain Forest People *(cont.)*

The People of the Amazon

Brazilian Beetle

The Brazilian beetle is a toy that originated in the rain forest of Brazil. It was very popular with the rain forest people between 1880 and 1910. It was also known as rattlesnake eggs and Tasmanian termite. This toy demonstrates potential and kinetic energy. Kinetic energy is energy that comes from the *motion* of an object. Potential energy is the *stored* energy in an object, for example, water in the reservoir behind a dam.

Enjoy making your Brazilian beetle "buzz" as you learn about potential and kinetic energy.

Activity

Materials:

- large metal paper clip
- thin rubber band
- large button with holes
- envelope
- small paper clip
- masking tape

Directions:

1. Open the large paper clip and shape it into a "U."
2. Bend the ends down and cover them with tape.
3. Thread the rubber band through two holes in the button.
4. Attach the rubber band to the paper clip.
5. Twist the button until the rubber band is tightly wound up. *This is potential energy.*
6. Carefully holding your Brazilian beetle, place it inside the envelope.
7. Close the envelope with the small paper clip.
8. Give the envelope to an unsuspecting person. When the envelope is opened, the beetle "buzzes." *This is kinetic energy.*

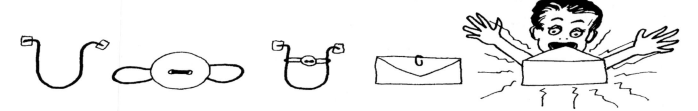

Challenge:

Create a toy, tool, or game using only the materials that would be available to you if you lived in a rain forest.

Rain Forest People *(cont.)*

Activities

❏ The government has decided to build a road right through the section of the rain forest where your people have always lived. This will drastically change your tribe's lifestyle forever. With a partner, write a conversation between the government official and your tribal chief. Be certain to use all of the proper punctuation in your written conversation. Use this conversation as the basis of a short skit to be presented to others.

❏ Mandrills are a species of monkey that live in the rain forest. They are known for their colorful face and groin areas. Mandrills talk to each other with grunts and sleep in trees, but, unfortunately, many of their trees are being cut down. In pairs, one being the mandrill and the other his interpreter, convey the mandrill's feelings about the loss of his trees.

❏ A myth is a traditional story often founded on some fact of nature or an event in the early history of a people. Many jungle myths have a common theme, wit against strength. Create your own jungle myth, or select your favorite one, to present as a puppet play. Old socks can be used to construct hand puppets by using felt, buttons, beads, yarn, material, and a lot of creativity.

❏ Da Ga (an African tag game called "Snake")— Choose an area about ten feet square (.93 m²) to be the "Home of the Snake." Pick one student to be the "Snake." The "Snake" starts from "Home" to catch another player by tagging him or her. When that person is caught, the two must hold hands and go on catching people, using their two free hands. The "Snake" will gradually become longer and longer as the game is played. Whenever the snake breaks, it must return to "Home," and a new "Snake" starts out to catch its victims. The game ends when all players are caught and become part of the snake. The last one caught is the winner.

❏ Jambo, Watatoe (Hello, Children)— The favorite games of African children are usually rhythmic and involve the use of stones. These games are played by passing stones around in a circle to a predetermined rhythm and chant. Each child finds a stone and marks it in some distinguishing way with a marker or paint. The object of the game is to keep in rhythm so that the stones come full circle (each player receives his own stone back). Use the following chant or make up your own.

"Jambo, Rafiki—Karibu" (Hello, Friend—Welcome)

Jambo—pick up stone in front of you

Rafiki—hold stone at your heart

Karibu—place stone in front of player to your right

❏ Rain Forest People— Create a rain forest "people" using natural materials you find in your yard or neighborhood. For instance, you could use a coconut or a pine cone for the head. Write a story about why it looks the way it does.

❏ Choose a rain forest tribe. Construct a diorama depicting a village scene.

Native News

You are a reporter for the *Native News*. Your job is to interview a native your own age who lives in one of the world's rain forests. You want to find out as much about this person as possible for the readers of the *Native News*. You know it is important for people of different cultures to know and understand each other. Use the questions below and any others that you think are relevant.

Activity

Choose a classmate to represent the rain forest native. Write your interview for the *Native News*. Rehearse your interview for a TV news show. (Make sure to research the answers to confirm that they are as accurate as possible before your broadcast.) When you are fully prepared, tape the interview.

Questions:

- What is your name?
- Does your name have a special meaning?
- Tell me about your family.
- What kind of chores are you responsible for?
- What do you do for fun?
- Describe your home.
- What is the weather like where you live?
- What do you and your family eat?
- What type of clothing do you wear?

- How do you get your food?
- What are your father's responsibilities?
- What are your mother's responsibilities?
- What is the best thing about living in the rain forest?
- What is the worst thing about living in the rain forest?
- What is special about your people?
- If you could send a message to children living outside the rain forest, what would it be?

Other Questions:

_____

_____

_____

_____

Write the answers to your questions on a separate sheet of paper as a rough draft. Next, using the following page, rewrite your rough draft as a newspaper interview for the *Native News*.

Native News

Volume One	Date:

Meet a Rain Forest Native
by: _____

_____

_____

_____

_____

_____

_____

_____

_____

_____

_____

_____

Rain Forest native, _____ , at

_____

_____

_____

_____

_____

Gifts from the Jungle

Although most of us live far from the world's rain forests, they touch our daily lives. If you have ever eaten a chocolate bar, sipped a cup of coffee or tea, or munched on a banana, then you have used a product that has its origins in the jungle. In the United States, we grow many citrus fruits, but did you know that oranges, grapefruits, and pineapples are all plants that originated in the rain forests?

Cacao trees, growing wild in the Amazon rain forest, provide us with chocolate. The chocolate comes from beans that grow in pods on this small tree. Although today most cocoa comes from large tree farms, the trees on the farms all originated in the rain forest. African kola nuts add flavor to many popular cola soft drinks. Chicle for chewing gum, durian fruit, and vanilla are just a few of the food products originally found in the jungle. Interestingly, nutmeg and mace are found in the same species of fruit. The mace comes from the red, net-like seed casing, and the nutmeg comes from the seed itself.

Manioc is a root that provides many people in tropical rain forests with their main source of starch. You may have eaten a product of the manioc root for dessert. What is it? Tapioca! Surprisingly, seeds of the red "lipstick" tree produce a yellow dye used for coloring soap, cheese, and even rubber.

Rubber, another product now grown on tree farms, has its origins in jungle trees. The tree's inner bark contains a liquid called latex. When the latex is heated or mixed with chemicals, tiny particles in the liquid stick together and form a solid lump of rubber.

The copaiba tree gives off a sap that is pure diesel oil. The difference between this fuel and other fossil fuels (gas, coal, oil) is that the tree will produce oil as long as it lives.

Ceiba is the scientific name for a large group of trees that grow to be 130 feet (40 meters) or more in height. The kapok tree belongs to this group. Its short, elastic fibers are used in making upholstery and floss. The seed oil of the kapok tree is used in the manufacture of soap. The fiber, or kapok, is water repellent. Large amounts of kapok are used to produce life preservers.

Science has shown us many reasons for protecting the earth's rain forests. Jungles can absorb the strong winds of tropical storms. Scientists believe that without the protection of the rain forests, tropical countries would suffer even greater damage when hurricanes and typhoons hit. Also, when the jungles have been cut down, the heavy rainfalls wash the soil into rivers even faster. In some countries, rivers are filling up with enough soil to create new islands. Scientists are worried, too, that if all the jungles are destroyed, we will never know about the many foods and useful medicines yet to be discovered.

Gifts from the Jungle *(cont.)*

What products that you use today do you think originated in the rain forest? There are more than you can imagine!

A wide variety of products that we use today originated in the tropical rain forests. There are woods, foods, oils, medicines, plants, fibers, spices, and other products. Take this list home and check off as many of these products as you can locate. You may need to look at product labels to correctly identify some items. Afterwards, compare your list with those of your classmates. Bring in a few of these products to make a classroom display to help educate others:

Fruits and Vegetables

_____ avocado	_____ lemon	_____ tangerine
_____ cucumber	_____ papaya	_____ coconut
_____ jackfruit	_____ rambutan	_____ guava
_____ orange	_____ breadfruit	_____ mango
_____ plantain	_____ grapefruit	_____ pineapple
_____ banana	_____ lime	_____ yam
_____ durian	_____ passion fruit	

Spices

_____ allspice	_____ cinnamon	_____ cayenne
_____ chili pepper	_____ nutmeg	_____ ginger
_____ mace	_____ cardamon	_____ turmeric
_____ vanilla	_____ cloves	
_____ black pepper	_____ paprika	

Other Foods

_____ Brazil nuts	_____ coffee	_____ peanuts
_____ chocolate	_____ okra	_____ tea
_____ manioc	_____ tapioca	_____ chayote
_____ sesame seed	_____ cashew nuts	_____ hearts of palm
_____ cane sugar	_____ cola	

Gifts from the Jungle *(cont.)*

See page 94 for directions.

Oils

_____ bay (perfume)

_____ camphor (perfume, soap, disinfectant, insect repellent, detergent)

_____ cascarilla (confectionery, beverages)

_____ coconut (suntan lotion, candles)

_____ eucalyptus (perfume, cough drops)

_____ guaiac (perfume)

_____ palm (shampoo, detergents, foods)

_____ patchouli (perfume)

_____ rosewood (perfume, cosmetics, flavorings)

_____ sandalwood (perfume)

_____ star anise (perfume, confectionery, beverages, cough drops)

_____ ylang-ylang (perfume)

Medicines

_____ curare (muscle relaxant for surgery)

_____ diosgenin (steroids, asthma, and arthritis treatment)

_____ quassia (insecticides)

_____ quinine (anti-malaria, pneumonia treatment)

_____ reserpine (sedative, tranquilizer)

_____ strophanthus (heart disease medicine)

_____ strychnine (insecticide, flea dip)

Woods

_____ balsa

_____ sandalwood

_____ mahogany

_____ teak

_____ rosewood

(Tropical woods are used in furniture, doors, window sills, flooring, paneling, veneer, cabinets, salad bowls, toys, insulation, plywood, and construction.)

Gifts from the Jungle *(cont.)*

See page 94 for directions.

Fibers

_____ bamboo (cane, furniture, crafts, baskets)

_____ jute (rope, twine, burlap)

_____ kapok (insulation, stuffing, life jackets, soundproofing)

_____ raffia (rope, cord, baskets)

_____ ramie (knit materials, fishing line)

_____ rattan (furniture, wicker, cane chair

Plants

_____ African violets

_____ begonia

_____ croton

_____ fiddle-leaf fig

_____ philodendron

_____ snake plant

_____ umbrella tree (schefflera)

_____ aluminum plant

_____ bromeliads

_____ dieffenbachia

_____ orchids

_____ prayer plant

_____ spathe lily

_____ anthurium

_____ Christmas cactus

_____ dracaena

_____ parlor ivy

_____ rubber tree plant

_____ Swiss cheese plant

_____ zebra plant

Other Products

_____ chicle (chewing gum)

_____ copaiba (perfume, fuel)

_____ copal (varnish, paint, printing ink)

_____ dammar (varnish, lacquer, printing ink)

_____ gutta percha (golf ball covers)

_____ rubber (balloons, erasers, foam rubber, balls, rubber bands, rubber cement, gloves, hoses, shoes, tires, rain gear)

Puzzling Products

Scientists found a puzzling list of rain forest products. Can you help make some sense of it? Look for hints on the lists of rain forest products.

1. nuoocct _____

2. aaaypp _____

3. lnaiavl _____

4. ntaalinp _____

5. gonam _____

6. may _____

7. ripaapk _____

8. hocird _____

9. aalbs _____

10. ekat _____

11. ynmaaogh _____

12. regnig _____

13. mucburec _____

14. nnnmoaic _____

15. papeipnel _____

16. cuepalusty _____

17. sisaauq _____

18. neneyac _____

19. domelabri _____

20. tailpouch _____

Going Bananas!

It is generally agreed that the banana originated in Malaysia and the East Indies. You may be surprised to know that bananas are actually berries. The scientific definition for a berry is a simple fruit having a skin surrounding one or more seeds in a fleshy pulp. Grapes, tomatoes, currants, and bananas are all classified as berries.

Bananas grow on a tropical plant that is not classified as a tree because it does not have a trunk. Instead, it is considered a gigantic herb that grows from an underground stem. It takes 15 to 18 months to grow the one stalk of bananas that each plant bears. Bananas on the stalk point upwards as they grow. After harvesting the bananas, the plant is cut down and the underground rootstock produces new shoots for the next plant.

There are over one hundred varieties of bananas. Pound for pound, bananas are the most widely sold fruit in the United States. Honduras, Panama, Ecuador, and Guatemala all ship bananas to the United States; however, Ecuador is the largest exporter of bananas. Bananas are a very convenient and nutritious food and come complete with their own wrapping.

Plantains, larger than common bananas and primarily used for cooking, are a staple food in the tropics. Plantains take the place of potatoes in some countries. Plantain chips are the tropical equivalent of potato chips.

Activities

Choose one or more of the following banana activities.

- Pretend that you are a monkey and that you have just found your very first banana. Pantomime what you would do and how you would react to your first taste.

- Read the book *The Day the Teacher Went Bananas* by James Howe. Write your own creative version of the story and illustrate it.

- Using the expression "Bananas Have Real Appeal," brainstorm methods of peeling bananas...without using your hands!

- Create Banana "Hink Pinks." A hink is a two-word answer to a riddle where the two words rhyme. For example: an adorable banana...cute fruit, a yearning for an ice cream treat...split fit, a banana's natural covering...real peel, and a delicious banana snack...sweet treat.

- Use the jungle products listed in the recipe on page 99 to make delicious Banana Bars.

Going Bananas! *(cont.)*

Banana bars combine three popular rain forest products, chocolate, bananas, and vanilla, into a delicious treat.

Ingredients:

- ³/₄ cup (180 mL) butter or margarine (1 ¹/₂ sticks)
- ²/₃ cup (165 mL) sugar
- ²/₃ cup (165 mL) packed brown sugar
- 1 egg
- 1 teaspoon (5 mL) vanilla
- 1 cup (240 mL) mashed ripe bananas (3 medium)
- 2 ¹/₄ cups (540 mL) all-purpose flour
- 2 teaspoons (10 mL) baking powder
- ¹/₂ teaspoon (2.5 mL) salt
- 16-ounce package (1 cup or 240 mL) semisweet chocolate pieces
- large mixing bowl
- medium mixing bowl
- electric mixer
- wooden spoon
- 15" x 10" x 1" (38 cm x 25 cm x 2.5 cm) baking pan

Directions:

1. Preheat oven to 350° F (180° C).
2. Grease baking pan with a little shortening.
3. In the large mixing bowl, beat butter or margarine with electric mixer on medium speed until softened.
4. Add sugar and brown sugar. Beat until fluffy.
5. Add egg and vanilla. Beat well.
6. Stir in mashed bananas.
7. In the medium mixing bowl, stir together flour, baking powder, and salt.
8. Using low speed on the mixer, gradually add the flour mixture to the banana mixture. Beat well until mixed.
9. Using a wooden spoon, stir in the chocolate pieces.
10. Spread the batter into the greased baking pan.
11. Bake in a preheated 350° F (180° C) oven about 25 minutes or until a toothpick inserted in the center comes out clean.
12. Cool pan on a cooling rack.
13. When cooled, cut into bars. Makes approximately 36 bars.

Heavenly Chocolate

Chocolate, America's favorite flavor, is a natural product made from the bean of a cacao tree. The cacao trees are grown in a belt-like area, 20° north and south of the equator, in Brazil, Central America, the Caribbean, Indonesia, and West Africa.

The Ivory Coast in West Africa is the largest seller of cacao beans and with Brazil grows nearly 45% of the world's cacao beans. The United States is the largest buyer of cacao beans and is the world leader in chocolate manufacturing. Switzerland is the leading chocolate consuming nation with a per person annual consumption of 22 pounds (10 kg), compared to 10.2 pounds (4.6 kg) per person annually in the United States.

Cacao beans are found in the hard pods of the tall cacao trees which can reach heights of 20 to 40 feet (6 to 12 m). Cacao trees bloom continuously, allowing pods from mature trees to be harvested monthly. Each pod is about 8 inches (20 cm) long and contains 20 to 50 beans. Once the beans are harvested, using machetes, they are removed from the pods and are fermented for approximately three to nine days. Afterwards, they are dried in the sun for about one week.

The dried beans are then packed and shipped to manufacturers where they are sorted and cleaned. Each manufacturer then blends and roasts the beans in a large rotary cylinder for up to two hours. It is during this process that the aroma, flavor, and dark brown color develop.

After roasting, the outer shells of the beans are removed. The beans are cracked into small pieces called nibs. The nibs are heated and ground into a paste, releasing their cocoa butter. The result of this process is called chocolate liquor or cocoa paste. Even though the paste is called chocolate liquor, it does not contain alcohol. This pure cocoa paste is poured into molds and then hardens after cooling. It is now unsweetened chocolate.

A very important step in the making of chocolate is the prolonged stirring in a large vat called a "conche." The "conche" (a Greek term meaning seashell) got its name many years ago because it is shaped like a giant seashell. This machine agitates and aerates the chocolate to give it a smooth texture. During this process, other ingredients such as sugar, vanilla, lecithin, dried milk, and other flavorings are added to the unsweetened chocolate. Next, the chocolate passes through steel rollers, ensuring its smoothness. The final step is to pour the chocolate into molds and allow it to cool.

Heavenly Chocolate *(cont.)*

Over two thousand years ago the Mayan culture used the cacao bean as a form of currency. In the early 1500s the Spanish explorer, Hernando Cortez, encountered the last Aztec emperor, Montezuma II, in Mexico. Cortez discovered that the Aztecs treated the cacao beans as priceless treasures. These cacao beans were used to make the drink, "cacahuatt." After Cortez tasted this unusual drink, he decided to bring it back to Spain where water and sweeteners were added to it.

The Spanish nobility kept this delicious formula a secret for many years. Eventually, the secret of the improved "cacahuatt" spread to other lands, and by the 1700s chocolate houses were as prominent as coffee houses in England. The rest is history!

Activities

- Write the letters of the alphabet down the side of a piece of paper. Beside each letter, write the name of a chocolate treat that starts with the letter listed. Use a cookbook, dictionary, or reference book for ideas.

- Find a recipe for a scrumptious chocolate dessert. Copy the recipe and include a drawing or a picture.

- Create an original chocolate treat: list the ingredients, directions, and an illustration.

- Give your creation a name. Design a wrapper for your original chocolate treat. Make sure to list the ingredients on the back of the wrapper.

- Write a radio or TV commercial for your new product.

- Create a poster or billboard advertisement for your new product.

- Chocolate treats may be made by the class and sold in the Rain Forest Museum (see Section VIII).

- Assemble a rain forest chocolate recipe book to be sold in the Rain Forest Museum (see Section VIII).

Resources:

- Film: *A Great American Chocolate Story,* 27 minutes, available free from Modern Talking Picture Service, 5000 Park Street North, St. Petersburg, FL 33709, Free Loan #18363

- This film offers an opportunity to learn about chocolate by taking a journey that begins in exotic countries and concludes with the familiar chocolate products sold in stores.

- Book: *Chocolate.* Teacher Created Resources, Inc., TCM #239
  This book is a thematic unit based entirely on the subject of chocolate.

Heavenly Chocolate *(cont.)*

Chocolate Quiz

Answer the following questions about chocolate.

1. What is the most important ingredient in chocolate?

   _____

2. Who was the Spanish explorer who took cacao beans back to Spain?

   _____

3. What plant do cacao beans come from?

   _____

4. Name five places where cacao beans grow.

   _____

   _____

5. What is a nib?

   _____

6. Which country sells the most cacao beans?

   _____

7. Where did the word "conche" come from?

   _____

   _____

8. What did the Mayans use cacao beans for?

   _____

9. What new chocolate drink was very popular in Spain?

   _____

10. What country is the largest buyer of chocolate?

   _____

Heavenly Chocolate *(cont.)*

Chocolate Challenge

Directions: All of the answers are the names of familiar chocolate candies. You have five minutes to figure out the name of the chocolate candy from the given clues. Then, you will have another five minutes to work with a partner to complete this challenge.

1. **Planet Closest to Earth** _____

2. **A Sweet Sign of Affection** _____

3. **Nut Happiness** _____

4. **Famous New York Street** _____

5. **Twin Letters** _____

6. **A Feline** _____

7. **Bite With Crackling Noise** _____

8. **Pleasingly Plump** _____

9. **Superman's Other Identity** _____

10. **Famous Former Baseball Player** _____

11. **Two Female Pronouns** _____

12. **A Famous Swashbuckling Trio of Old** _____

13. **Can't Hold on to Anything** _____

14. **Indian Burial Grounds** _____

15. **Not Laughing out Loud** _____

16. **Galaxy** _____

17. **Favorite Day for Working People** _____

18. **Sweet Infants** _____

Bouncing Rubber

Rubber comes from the juice of the hevea, a rain forest tree we call the rubber tree. One of the countries it grows in is Brazil. Natural latex seeps out of the tree when it is cut, much like soap (for maple syrup) does from maple trees in northern climates. Rubber trappers make their living by collecting the latex in cups from the many rubber trees found in the forest. Rubber is considered an "extractive" resource because it can be removed without damaging the tree. Other products that can be removed without damage to the rain forest are chicle (used to make chewing gum), rattan, palm oil, wicker, flowers of the ylang-ylang (perfume), cashews, and Brazil nuts.

Activity

You can find natural rubber, or latex, in certain common plants. Take a walk in your neighborhood and collect some wild dandelions, goldenrod, or milkweed pods. Break the stems and leaves of the plants and squeeze. The white sap that oozes out is a form of latex.

Squeeze out enough sap to coat your fingertip. Allow the sap to dry until it is colorless. Next, roll the substance off your finger. What happens when you stretch it? (It pulls back to its original shape.) When you rub it on a pencil mark? (It erases the mark.) What if you rolled it into a ball and dropped it? (It would bounce.) In other words, it would act just like the latex of the hevea tree from the rain forest.

In the following activity, you will learn to make latex into a rubber ball.

Materials: (per person)

- 1 teaspoon (15 mL) latex
- paper cup
- 1 tablespoon (15 mL) water
- 1 tablespoon (15 mL) vinegar
- 2–3 drops food coloring (any color)
- craft stick
- paper towel
- plastic sandwich bag

Directions:

1. Pour latex into a paper cup. Dip the end of your finger into the latex and notice how it feels. (Teacher Note: Latex is not a hazardous chemical. It can be purchased at art supply stores.)

2. Stir water into the latex with a wooden craft stick.

Bouncing Rubber *(cont.)*

Directions: *(cont.)*

3. Add 2–3 drops of food coloring.

4. Stir the mixture again with the craft stick.

5. Add the vinegar to the mixture and stir. Observe the mixture carefully as you add the vinegar.

6. You have now made rubber! Wash the hardened mixture carefully in the sink to remove any extra latex or vinegar. Vinegar is a mild acid and may sting if it touches a cut. Simply rinse the area with water.

7. Dry the ball carefully. Now drop the ball onto the floor. What happened?

    Your rubber ball can be preserved in the plastic bag.

Challenge:

1. Think about how the latex looked, felt, and smelled in the process of making rubber. Now create a story about this process, adding as many details as possible. Be sure to include a description of the rubber ball you made and the way the ball behaved when dropped.

2. Make a list of the ways that rubber is used today.

3. Imagine that suddenly there is a worldwide shortage of rubber. What could we use as a substitute?

4. Research rubber production from start of finish. Share your information in a series of pictures with captions. Be sure to include collecting latex, exporting latex, transportation to seaports for shipping, what happens when the ship arrives at its destination, and manufacturing with rubber.

5. Use your homemade rubber balls in bouncing contests with your classmates. Compete in the areas of height, distance, and number of bounces. After the contests, investigate why the winners won. Did the size of the ball matter? Did the shape make a difference? Is there a special technique used in expert ball bouncing? Think of some of your own investigative questions.

6. Take a "Sole Poll." Take a poll of what materials are used to make the soles of your shoes. Check your closet for all the soles made with rubber, plastic, leather, wood, etc. You may wish to extend your investigation to the shoes of your entire family. Chart your findings.

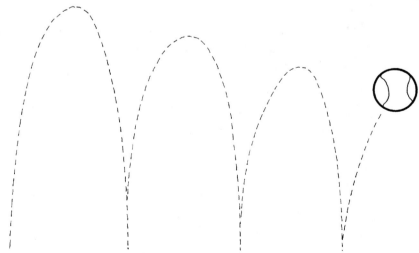

Tropical Treats

Create your own recipe for a tropical treat using your knowledge about foods from the rain forests. In addition, plan a one-day menu using as many tropical foods as possible. The following are some recipes to help spark your imagination.

Fruity Rain Forest Fantasy

Ingredients:
- oranges
- pineapple
- mangos
- grapes
- bananas

Fruit Dip:
- 1–8 oz. (237 mL) package cream cheese (softened)
- 6 oz. (177 mL) marshmallow creme
- 1 tablespoon (15 mL) orange juice
- 1 pinch of ground ginger

Directions:
1. Peel, slice, and divide the oranges, pineapple, bananas and mangos. Arrange the grapes and other fruit on a plate.
2. To make the dip, use an electric mixer (at medium speed). Beat together all of the dip ingredients until well blended.
3. Use toothpicks to hold the fruit while dipping.

Choco-Nut Treat

Ingredients:
- ½ cup (120 mL) cashews
- ½ cup (120 mL) Brazil nuts
- ½ cup (120 mL) peanuts
- ½ cup (120 mL) macadamia nuts
- 1 cup (240 mL) broken banana chips
- 1 cup (240 mL) chocolate chips
- 1 cup (240 mL) dried pineapple chunks
- ½ cup (120 mL) coconut flakes

Directions:
1. Combine all the ingredients into a large mixing bowl.
2. Enjoy your choco-nut treat!

Jungle Juice

Ingredients:
- 1 banana (ripe)
- 1 cup (240 mL) strawberries
- 1 cup (240 mL) orange juice
- 1 cup (240 mL) pineapple juice
- 1 pint (470 mL) vanilla ice cream
- 1 can lemon-lime soda

Directions:
1. Place the ripe banana and strawberries in a blender to purée.
2. Add the orange and pineapple juice and blend together.
3. Put ice cream into a punch bowl.
4. Pour juice mixture into punch bowl on top of the ice cream.
5. Add the lemon-lime soda to the punch bowl.

Snake Stew for You?

Africa has a great diversity of food types. A visitor could experience some very unusual foods. Feel like chewing gum? Why not try some kola nuts instead. You may be served some fou-fou which is made from white yams. Are you feeling daring today? Try some larva or fried snake for lunch. Termites or roasted grubs make a tasty snack.

Some African foods are not so exotic. You can cook up one of their favorite snacks of fried bananas sprinkled with sugar and cinnamon. Some native African foods can be found in your neighborhood supermarket, such as papaya, lichees, mangoes, yams, avocados, and figs.

Activity

Create an original recipe for snake stew. What ingredients would you use? List the ingredients and amounts. Write the step-by-step directions to make snake stew. Draw an illustration for your recipe on a separate piece of paper and share it with the class.

Snake Stew

Ingredients:

_____   _____

_____   _____

_____   _____

_____   _____

Directions:

_____

_____

_____

_____

_____

_____

Tropical Sense-sations

An ancient Chinese proverb tells us this:

I see and I forget
I hear and I remember
I do and I understand

The following activities use the senses to identify products from the rain forest.

Touch

Use an old pillow case to make a touchy-feely game. Each day, place a different product that originates in the rain forest into the bag. Students must identify the object using only their sense of touch. Have students write their guesses on a piece of paper and place them into a decorated box. When each student has had a turn, tally the guesses.

Display the item. How many students guessed correctly? Repeat this activity using different items. Some suggested items are:

- chewing gum
- chocolate
- rubber eraser

- chopsticks
- tea bag
- wicker or rattan basket

- peanut
- yam
- banana

Additionally, items can be taken from the list of rain forest products.

Smell

Use empty film canisters (35 mm film size), small, thinly woven cloth squares, rubber bands, and various fragrant rain forest products to make this scent-sational activity. Put a small amount of the fragrant item into the canister. Cover it with a cloth square and use a rubber band to hold the cloth in place. Some suggested fragrant items are:

- cinnamon
- coffee
- cloves
- nutmeg
- ginger

- tea
- lemon peel
- chocolate
- pineapple
- black pepper

- vanilla
- peanut
- coconut

Students will use only their sense of smell to identify the item in the canister.

Taste

Place tropical morsels onto the tongues of blindfolded students. By using only their sense of taste, they must identify the items. Suggested tasting items:

- orange
- banana
- lemon

- grapefruit
- avocado
- sugar

- sesame seeds
- cucumber
- yam

Matrix Puzzle

For every letter given in the left column, think of a rain forest animal, food, plant, product, and word which begins with that letter. In a group, have a competition to see who can fill as many spaces as possible on the grid.

Sample:

	Animal	Food	Plant	Products	Rain Forest Words
B	bush baby	banana	bromeliad	bamboo	buttress

	Animal	Food	Plant	Products	Rain Forest Words
F					
O					
R					
E					
S					
T					

Scoring Suggestions: If only one person has a specific answer (for example: an F animal is a ferret) he/she receives five points; two to three people with the same answer each receive three points; four or more people with the same answer each receive one point. Each student adds up his or her points, and the highest number of points wins.

People and Products Brain Strain

This problem has only one solution. To fill in the chart, mark an "X" in each square which is eliminated by a clue. When there is only one blank square left in a row or column within a category, put a happy face in that square.

Activity

The following rain forest people, Kebe (KEH-bay), Alita (ah-LEE-ta), Ima (EE-mah), and Alukulu (ah-LOO-koo-loo) chose the following rain forest products for their dinners—banana, mango, chocolate, and cashew nuts. Read the clues below to discover what each person chose.

Clues:

1. Alukulu, Ima, and the person who likes chocolates are best friends.

2. Ima and Alita are allergic to mangos.

3. Ima and Alukulu do not like nuts.

4. Alukulu and the person who chose the chocolate have names that begin with the same letter.

People and Products Brain Strain Chart

	Banana	Mango	Chocolate	Cashew nuts
Kebe				
Alita				
Ima				
Alukulu				

Poet-Tree

This section focuses on creative writing about the rain forest through the use of poetry.

The Rain Forest Poet

Creative expression is an essential aspect of any multi-dimensional thematic unit. The poetry can be used to express feelings about the beauty of the rain forest, the harmony that exists between people and their environment, and the plight of the vanishing rain forest.

Suggestions for Extending the Section:

- Cut various rain forest leaf shapes out of construction paper. Each form of poetry can be displayed on a different shaped leaf. These leaves can be used to decorate your classroom.

- A Poet-Tree: Writing generated from this section can be placed on a rain forest tree as a wall display.

- Leafy Lines: Cut out a rain forest leaf pattern. Use this pattern to create the pages of a poetry book. Patterns found in the museum section (Section VIII) of this book can be used as samples. Place a different rain forest poem on each page of the book. Use the method of your choice to bind the book.

- Create illustrations for the poetry in this section.

- Using a tune of your choice, make your poetry into a song.

- Using other poetic forms, create additional poems.

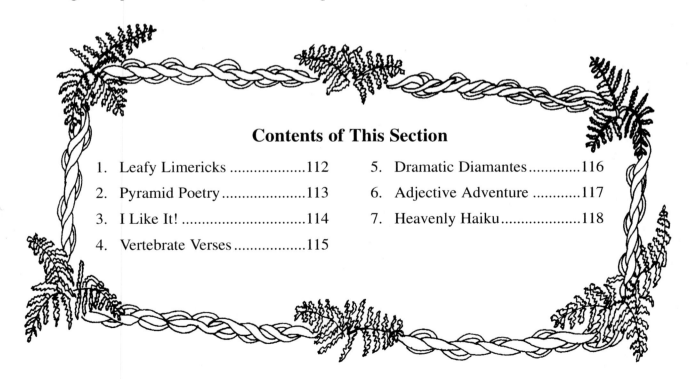

Contents of This Section

Leafy Limericks

A limerick is a five-line poem with a specific rhyming pattern and syllable pattern. Lines 1, 2, and 5 rhyme and have eight syllables each. Lines 3 and 4 rhyme and have five syllables each.

Example:

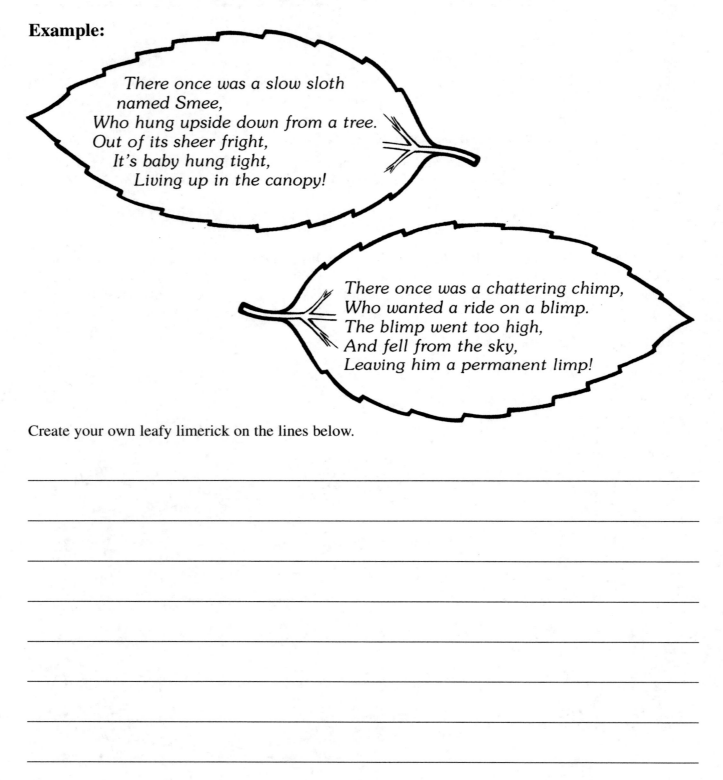

*There once was a slow sloth
named Smee,
Who hung upside down from a tree.
Out of its sheer fright,
It's baby hung tight,
Living up in the canopy!*

*There once was a chattering chimp,
Who wanted a ride on a blimp.
The blimp went too high,
And fell from the sky,
Leaving him a permanent limp!*

Create your own leafy limerick on the lines below.

_____

_____

_____

_____

_____

_____

_____

Pyramid Poetry

Pyramid poetry gets its name from its shape, a pyramid. It follows a specific form consisting of six lines.

Line 1: one word title

Line 2: two words describing how the word in line 1 *smells*

Line 3: three words describing how the word in line 1 *sounds*

Line 4: four words describing what the word in line 1 *looks* like

Line 5: five words describing how the word in line 1 *feels* to the touch

Line 6: six words stating your opinion or inner feelings about the word in line 1

Example:

Snake
Musky, Earthy,
Swooshing, Silent, Hissing,
Bendable, Dangerous, Rope-like, Glossy,
Cool, Smooth, Scaley, Strong, Hard,
Useful Animals to the Rain Forest.

Create your own pyramid poem using the lines below.

_____

_____ , _____ ,

_____ , _____ , _____ ,

_____ , _____ , _____ , _____ ,

_____ , _____ , _____ , _____ , _____ ,

_____ _____ _____ _____ _____ _____ .

I Like It!

The following poem states the author's opinion. Try writing an "I Like It" poem patterned after this one.

Example:

> *The rain forest is a beautiful place,*
> *I like it!*
> *It always shows its emerald face,*
> *I like it!*
> *It's the place where the animals play.*
> *It always takes my breath away.*
> *In the rain forest, I'd like to stay.*
> *I like it!*

_____

_____

_____

_____

_____

_____

_____

_____

_____

_____

_____

_____

Vertebrate Verses (Spine Poems)

Vertebrate Verses use the concepts of simile and metaphor.

A simile is a comparison between two often unrelated things. They are always compared by using the words *like* or *as*.

> **Example:** The jungle birds were *like* bright, chattering flowers.
>
> The dolphin was as sleek *as* a submarine in the water.
>
> A metaphor does the same thing as a simile, but does not use the words like or as.
>
> **Example:** The ants on the leaves were an invading army.
>
> The canopy is an umbrella over the rain forest.

The vertebrate verse does not have to rhyme. Once you have decided upon your simile or metaphor, place one word per line directly under each other, creating a straight line, much like the vertebrate (spine) of an animal. Read the example below. Then, write your own simile or metaphor.

Ants

scurry

across

the

forest

floor

like

busy

shoppers

at

holiday

time!

Now give it a try:

_____

_____

_____

_____

_____

_____

_____

_____

Dramatic Diamantes

The diamante follows a specific format, and the finished poem takes the shape of a diamond. The diamante has seven lines and the form is as follows:

Line 1: Write a noun. (At this point you may wish to skip down to line 7 and write the antonym (opposite) of this noun.

Line 2: Write two adjectives describing the noun in line 1.

Line 3: Write three verbs (action words) ending in *-ing* that describe the noun.

Line 4: Write four nouns. The first two should relate to the noun in line 1 and the second two relate to the noun in line 7. Separate the pairs with a star.

Line 5: Write three verbs (action words) ending in *-ing* that describe the noun in line 7.

Line 6: Write two adjectives that describe the noun in line 7.

Line 7: Write a noun that is the antonym (opposite) of the noun in line 1.

Example:

Canopy
Noisy, Leafy
Buzzing, Chirping, Twittering
Birds, Epiphytes, Ants, Scorpions
Slithering, Scurrying, Decaying
Dark, Damp
Floor

Now, try to write your own diamante on the lines below. Be sure to follow the form described above.

_____

_____

_____

_____

_____

_____

_____

Adjective Adventure

The Adjective Adventure is a poem form. It consists of five lines. Lines 2 and 4 should rhyme.

Line 1: A one-word noun

Line 2: Four adjectives describing the noun in line 1

Line 3: Three additional adjectives describing the noun in line 1

Line 4: Four more adjectives describing the noun in line 1

Line 5: Three more adjectives describing the noun in line 1

Example:

Rain
Beating, drumming, wet, dreary,
Sloshing, pouring, sprinkling,
Annoying, misting, drenching, weary,
Pelting, splashing, damp.

Write your own Adjective Adventure using the given guidelines.

_____

_____

_____

_____

Heavenly Haiku

Haiku is a form of Japanese poetry. It usually focuses on the beauty of nature. In the 1660s, a poet named Matuso Basho wrote haiku and became responsible for making it a serious art form. Haiku poetry has a very unique style. A poem consists of 17 non-rhyming syllables organized into three lines in the following way:

Line 1: 5 syllables—   **Line 2:** 7 syllables—   **Line 3:** 5 syllables—

The haiku uses words to create a mood or feeling about a scene or setting from nature. The haiku poem suggests a time, place, and special quality of the poem's subject.

Activity

Follow the steps below to create your own haiku poetry about the beauty of the rain forest.

1. Study pictures of rain forest scenes or animals and discuss their beauty.

2. Create a list of words or phrases that describe where the scene takes place.

    Examples: in the forest, in the treetops, in the jungle, along the river

3. Create a list of phrases describing what is happening.

    Examples: rain is falling, water is rushing, birds are chirping, branches are swaying

4. Create a list of words that describe when it is happening.

    Examples: every day, in the spring, at sunrise, at midday

5. Join the words or phrases into Haiku form, adjusting syllables where necessary, to make sure that they match the guidelines given. Read the following haiku poem.

> Along the river
> Branches swaying up above
> Spring is in the air

6. On a separate piece of paper, write your own haiku poem using the guidelines given above.

Focus on Rain Forest Destruction

Problems and Solutions

This section focuses on the reasons tropical rain forests are being destroyed and examines some of the ways these forests can be protected.

Our Loss

For over one hundred million years, the rain forests have been like a living museum. One can find plants and animals there that have disappeared elsewhere in the world. Due to rapid deforestation, our rain forests are now in danger. The problems of the disappearing rain forests come from loss of trees due to farming, logging, ranching, and new development. Some theorize that one of the main reasons for global warming is deforestation. Our earth is a delicate ecosystem and what happens to one area of the earth affects the entire earth. We must work together to keep the rain forests alive.

Suggestions for Extending the Section

- Have students research and discuss why the ozone layer is being damaged. How will this affect the rain forest? What can we do to help change this trend?

- Allow students to role-play rain forest natives. Have them act or write about their feelings as they watch their forest home being destroyed.

Contents of This Section

Why Save the Rain Forests?

Rain Forest Facts

There are hundreds of very important reasons for saving the rain forests. Listed below are some of the most crucial ones.

1. Native people are losing their lands. Along with this loss of land comes the loss of their unique culture.

2. The burning of the rain forests releases carbon into the air. This carbon changes into carbon dioxide and may contribute to global warming.

3. The world's weather patterns could be changed by destroying tropical rain forests. Water from the forests evaporates to make rain.

4. The loss of thousands of acres of tropical rain forests causes local soil erosion and water pollution.

5. People around the world rely upon products from the rain forest, such as hardwoods and foods (bananas, coffee, and cocoa, for example).

6. Tropical rain forests are home to more than 50% of the earth's species of plants and animals.

7. Forty percent of the medicines in use today originally came from the rain forest.

8. Many species of migratory birds, including the North American songbirds, migrate to the tropical regions to avoid harsh winter weather.

9. Artists, scientists, and others have been drawn to the exotic and unique tropical rain forests.

10. The native people's unequaled knowledge of the plants, animals, and cycles of the rain forest would be lost forever.

Divide the class into cooperative groups of three or four students. Each group should choose two or three facts for discussion. What would the consequences be from each of the above if the rain forests were destroyed? Each group should present its information to the class, using their choice of format (posters, commercials, skits, etc.).

Are You Using Up Our Rain Forests?

The American consumer uses many products from the rain forest. Some are replenishable resources while others are not. Many of the products we use come from trees. Although it is true that not all paper products originate in the tropical rain forests, many do.

Activity

Try the following experiment to demonstrate the use of forest products by the American consumer.

Materials:

- plastic trash bags (one per student)
- bathroom scale

Activity:

1. Each student receives a plastic bag to collect all the paper that would normally be thrown away in one day at home.

2. The teacher should use one bag to collect all the paper that would normally be thrown away in the classroom in one day.

3. The bags should be weighed at the end of a 24-hour period. This figure can be used as the average paper waste for one day.

4. Calculate how much paper one family discards during a week, a month, a year.

5. The current population of the United States is about 240 million. Calculate the amount of paper discarded by the population each week, month, and year.

- How does this information relate to the deforestation of the tropical rain forests?

- Do you feel that you could use less paper? How?

- How could the average American use less paper?

- How does your family's paper consumption compare to other people's in your class?

- How does your class's paper consumption compare to other classes' consumption?

The Greenhouse Effect

The greenhouse effect is a naturally occurring phenomenon where the atmosphere of the earth traps heat from the sun. The atmosphere that allows sunlight through to warm the surface of the earth also traps the heat that is created. This warming of the earth is what allows life to exist.

The rain forests play an important part in preventing the earth's average temperature from rising higher than it is now. Some gases, especially carbon dioxide, methane, and the chloroflourocarbons used in refrigerant work to trap heat within the earth's atmosphere. The higher the concentration of these gases in the atmosphere, the warmer the Earth's climate will become.

The tropical rain forests offer a large resource of carbon. Plants take in carbon dioxide from the air and use it for both making food and growing. When a tree dies or is burned, the carbon in its tissues is released back into the air in the form of carbon dioxide. If that tree is replaced by another, the new tree will absorb an equal amount of carbon dioxide from the air as it grows. If, however, a large number of trees are not replaced, huge amounts of carbon will be released as carbon dioxide into the air. All this carbon will add to the amount of greenhouse gases present in the Earth's atmosphere.

Many scientists agree that about one quarter of the carbon dioxide being released into the air comes from the burning of the rain forests. In 1989 alone, the burning of the Brazilian forests possibly added 350 million tons of carbon to our atmosphere.

If the amount of carbon dioxide in the air doubles, the average world temperature would rise about 4.5%. Many people fear that this would cause the ice caps over Greenland, and possibly Antarctica, to melt. This, in turn, would cause sea levels to rise. Many low coastal lands around the world would become flooded. In some places, the heat could cause droughts which could destroy major crops.

Some scientists do not agree with the theory that the climate will become warmer due to greenhouse gases. They believe that it is possible that, as the temperature rises more water will evaporate from the oceans. This would result in so many clouds that it might block out sunlight, resulting in a decrease in the Earth's temperature.

The important question to ask yourself is this: Do we want to chance adding long-term damage to the climate by clearing rain forests? Would it be wiser to play it safe and keep our options open for the future? The countries that will make the ultimate decision on this issue are the rain forest countries themselves.

Challenge:

1. How does burning a forest harm the environment?

2. Research how much the Earth's average temperature has changed in the last 100 years. Make a chart using this information.

The Greenhouse Effect *(cont.)*

This experiment will create a model that shows how carbon dioxide and water vapor affect the rate at which the Earth loses heat (global warming).

Activity

Materials:

- hot water
- 2 glass jars
- 2 thermometers
- clear plastic wrap

Directions:

1. Carefully pour hot water into each of the glass jars until they are about two-thirds full.

2. Put a thermometer into each jar.

3. Quickly cover one of the jars and its thermometer with a sheet of clear plastic wrap. Be certain that the jar is well sealed.

4. Make a chart (similar to the sample below) to record your observations. Label the columns: Time Elapsed, Wrapped Jar, Unwrapped Jar.

Time Elapsed	Wrapped Jar	Unwrapped Jar
0		
2		

5. Record the starting temperature of each jar on your chart.

6. Predict which container will keep the water hot longer.

7. Record the temperature of the water in each jar every two minutes for the next 14 minutes.

8. Which of the two jars of water lost the most heat?

_____

9. Why do you think the other jar of water lost less heat?

_____

_____

10. Assume that water vapor and carbon dioxide in the atmosphere are similar to plastic wrap. What effect would they have on the earth's tempertures?

_____

_____

Madagascar Is Missing

Separated from Africa 165 million years ago, Madagascar became an isolated world. It boasts 10,000 kinds of flowering plants, including nearly a thousand unique species of orchids. Almost 400 species of amphibians and reptiles have evolved into creatures unlike any found elsewhere on this Indian Ocean island.

Malagasy, as islanders are called, are descended from African and Indonesian seagoers who arrived about 1,500 years ago. These frontier people have always battled wilderness and poverty. Sadly, four-fifths of Madagascar is now barren land, burned by farmers and cattle herders. When it rains, the hills of Madagascar "bleed" red clay into the sea.

Coffee, cloves, sisal, and vanilla are the chief exports of Madagascar. Eighty percent of the worldwide demand for vanilla is grown here. Vanilla is the essential ingredient in cola drinks and vanilla ice cream. Many villages depend on this export for their cash income.

The Malagasys' survival relies on the fact that 85% of them work in agriculture. Transportation is severely limited, roads are in disrepair, and most people still travel by oxcart. Malnutrition is widespread, and the average life expectancy is only 50 years.

Wealth and prestige are measured by cattle among the Malagasy. The 10 million cattle are a major source of strain on the environment; nevertheless; they are an integral part of Malagasy life and customs.

Until recently a male could not pass into manhood unless he stole cattle. As of today, a man still cannot marry without payment of cows for his bride. Cattle are killed and eaten only at funerals or other ceremonial occasions.

Prairie fires are intentionally set to clear land to provide food for the grazing herds. These fires often spread into the forests, reducing the Malagasys' main source of firewood. Ironically, due to the steadily falling per person income, most Malagasy are too poor to buy the kerosene that they use to cook their daily rice. Instead, they are substituting charcoal, made by cutting down and roasting trees. Charcoal burners pose an incredible threat to Madagascar's forests. As the forest is destroyed for cattle land and fuel, with it goes an untold number of possible drugs, barely studied for their potential health benefits. Native healers use folk remedies to cure everything from plague and malarial fevers to dandruff. The rosy periwinkle, found only on the island of Madagascar, is used to produce drugs for childhood leukemia.

The rain forests of Madagascar are competing with poverty and charcoal burners for their very survival.

Challenge:

After reading the information provided on this page and on page 125, complete the Reaction Sheet on page 126.

Chico Mendes...Rain Forest Hero (1944-1988)

Francisco "Chico" Mendes Filho was born in the Seringal Cachoeira, a part of the Brazilian rain forest that has many wild rubber trees. Chico's family had been rubber tappers for generations in the state of Acre, near the border of Peru and Bolivia, in the far western regions of Amazonia.

In 1969, the Brazilian government began a costly road-building and colonization program called the National Integration Program. It was designed to bring outside people into the heart of the rain forest. The government offered incentives to many of the poor people living in the populated eastern region of the country to relocate in the rain forest. They also tried to get large investors to establish cattle ranches deep in the rain forest.

As settlers and ranchers came to clear the rain forest land in Acre, the rubber tappers were forced to relocate. Most of them did as they were told and simply left the forest. Chico Mendes refused to go. He explained to his fellow tappers that they had rights, and he began to organize them to resist the relocation efforts of the government.

Chico thought of a plan to resist the government's efforts. He would have two hundred to three hundred families of rubber tappers form a line to block the bulldozers that were on their way to clear the forest. This type of protest is called passive resistance. Over the course of thirteen years, Chico organized 45 blockades and is reported to have saved close to three million acres of rain forest.

Chico established the Rural Worker's Union and was elected town councilman in Xapuri. Some people did not agree with what Chico was doing, and his life was threatened many times.

As time went on, Chico's reputation for trying to stop the destruction of the rain forest became internationally known. Instead of the roads and ranches that the government wanted, Chico suggested "extractive reserves." These are areas set aside for sustainable use by rubber tappers and gatherers of nuts, fruits, and fibers. Chico succeeded in getting the government to set aside about 5 million acres for this purpose.

Through the use of blockades and lobbying, Chico was able to set up an extractive reserve in the Seringal Cachoeira, the part of the forest where he was born and raised. This land had been bought by Darci Alves, a local rancher, who was suspected of a number of murders. Darci had made it known that he wanted to kill Chico.

One night in December of 1988, Chico walked out of his back door into the backyard. A shotgun blast was heard, and suddenly Chico lay dead on the ground. Darci Alves, the son of the rancher Darci, confessed to killing Chico.

Chico Mendes has left a lasting impression on the world. His lifelong work in saving the rain forest will not be forgotten.

Reaction Sheet

After reading the information on pages 124 and 125, respond to the following questions and statements.

1. Describe the situation in Madagascar. What are some of the problems facing the people of Madagascar?

    _____

    _____

2. Brainstorm some possible solutions to the problems in Madagascar. Write your ideas here:

    _____

    _____

3. Who was Franscisco "Chico" Mendes Filho?

    _____

    _____

4. Describe the situation in Brazil that prompted Chico's active role in saving the rain forest.

    _____

    _____

5. If you were Chico, what would you have done? Can you suggest another alternative to this problem?

    _____

    _____

6. Brainstorm ways in which people can do their part to save the rain forest. Write your ideas here:

    _____

    _____

    _____

    _____

The Forest on Film

Now that you have learned so much about the tropical rain forests and their plight, it is time to take action. It is necessary to teach others about the importance of saving our disappearing rain forests.

Activity

In cooperative groups, create a slide show or film strip presentation about the problems and solutions associated with the tropical rain forests of the world.

Materials for Slides:

- one sheet of thermal transparency film
- 2" x 2" (5 cm x 5 cm) Slide Grid Sheet (page 129)
- 2" x 2" (5 cm x 5 cm) super slide frames (available at your local camera store)
- permanent markers
- overhead markers
- scissors
- slide projector
- thermocopy machine

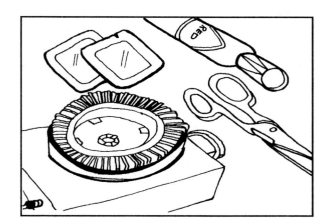

Directions for Slides:

1. Look at the 2" x 2" (5 cm x 5 cm) Slide Grid Sheet. The solid line portions of the squares are designed to be cut out and placed in the 2" x 2" super slide frame. The dotted portion of the square indicates the maximum area allowed for the message or picture that will be placed in the frame area.

2. Use a soft lead pencil to complete at least ten frames. You can use words and/or drawings on each frame. The pencil marks should be bold and clear. It may be necessary to darken the printing or drawing after the initial tracing.

3. When your frames are completed, use the thermocopy machine to produce a transparency.

4. Use permanent markers or overhead markers to color the completed frames.

5. Cut the transparency film on the solid lines of the grid and mount the printed material into a super slide frame. Load the slide frames into a projector and preview the product.

6. Show the slides to other classes to teach them about the plight of the disappearing rain forest.

Challenge:

- Write a script for narrating each slide of your presentaion.

The Forest on Film *(cont.)*

Materials for Filmstrip:

- blank 35 mm film strip
- permanent markers

Directions for making filmstrips:

1. Since the filmstrip is a fixed sequence media, the images and words must be drawn in the proper sequence on the 35 mm film. A single length of 35 mm film must be used. This can be ordered from: Highsmith Co., Inc., W5527 Highway 106, P.O. Box 800, Fort Atkinson, WI, 53538-0800. You can also produce your own by washing an old filmstrip or section of film with a solution of one-half water and one-half bleach.

2. Permanent markers can be used to draw and write on the film. Location of the drawing area, known as the frame, is difficult since there are no frame divisions on the film The filmstrip frame is the area between four adjacent sprocket holes.

3. Make certain to leave enough empty frames to allow it to be loaded into the projector. Also, add a focus frame at the beginning.

Note the number of sprocket holes for each frame. There are no frame lines in blank 35 mm film.

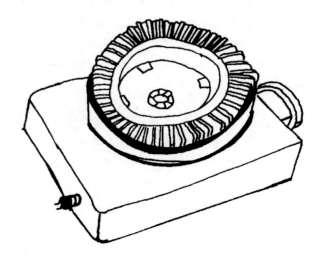

The Forest on Film *(cont.)*
Slide Grid Sheet

Rain Forest Crossword

Use the clues and word list on this page to complete the puzzle on page 131.

Word List

bromeliad	epiphyte	nutrients
canopy	equator	pollen
conservation	food chain	predator
deforestation	liana	savanna
ecology	nectar	shrubs
endangered species	nocturnal	understory

Across Clues

2. foliage layer beneath the main canopy of a forest
5. flow of food among different groups of organisms
7. animal that hunts other animals for food
9. tropical plant of the pineapple family
12. woody vine that is rooted in the soil and grows up tree trunks
14. bushy plants with woody stems
15. overhead layer of the forest made by the tops of tall trees
17. powder-like microspores produced by flowers
18. sugary fluid secreted by plants

Down Clues

1. stripping an area of trees and other vegetation
3. flat grassland in tropical regions
4. animals or plants that are threatened with extinction
6. vitamins and minerals necessary for life
8. preservation and protection of something
10. study of the environment
11. imaginary line halfway between the North and South poles
13. animals that are active at night and rest during the day
16. plant that grows on another plant without harming it

Rain Forest Crossword

Directions: Use the clues and word list on page 130 to compete this puzzle.

Rain Forest Museum

This section focuses on creating an educational culminating activity which demonstrates creative thinking, problem solving, and research skills.

"When we try to pick out one thing by itself, we find it hitched to everything else in the universe."

John Muir

The Importance of Knowledge

The world's rain forests need our help! Knowledge and understanding of the plight of the world's disappearing rain forests is the first step in preserving them. The knowledge that you have accumulated through the study of this unit can be transferred to others through action. Imagine redesigning your classroom, corridor, or entire school into a tropical rain forest museum, complete with trees, vines, unique plants, animals, and insects. This section contains instructions on how to create a rain forest museum and details on setting up a museum gift shop and ideas for fund-raising. Money raised can be used to purchase acreage for preservation of the world's rain forests.

Suggestions for Extending the Section:

- Advertise the coming of your rain forest museum by designing and creating posters to be hung around your school and community. Brainstorm some slogans to place on your posters, for example: Save the Rain Forest; May the Rain Forest Be With You; Rain, Rain, Don't Go Away; Going, Going, Gone?

- Create and wear advertising buttons. These buttons can be worn by students before the museum opens for promotional purposes and can also be sold in the gift shop.

Contents of This Section

Museum Options

There are many ways of setting up a rain forest museum. Several options will be provided. Choose the option that best fits your needs. Be sure to consider the following: Where can it be located? How big should it be? What should it include? How can we accomplish this? How can we best create the feeling of a rain forest?

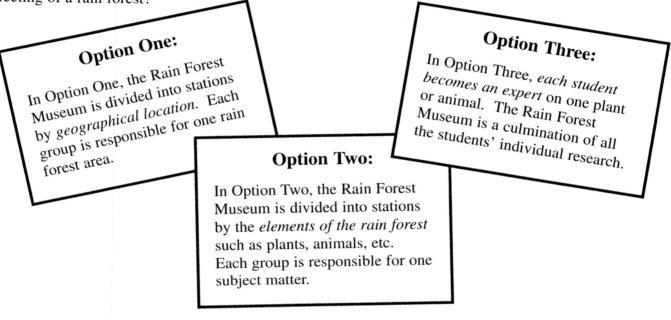

Option One:

In Option One, the Rain Forest Museum is divided into stations by *geographical location*. Each group is responsible for one rain forest area.

Option Three:

In Option Three, *each student becomes an expert* on one plant or animal. The Rain Forest Museum is a culmination of all the students' individual research.

Option Two:

In Option Two, the Rain Forest Museum is divided into stations by the *elements of the rain forest* such as plants, animals, etc. Each group is responsible for one subject matter.

Option One

Organized by Geographical Location

Overview:

Divide the rain forests of the world into geographical groups; for example, Africa, Asia, Central America, South America, Madagascar. Allow students to choose a geographical area. Organize students into cooperative groups of about four for each station (geographical area). Have each group elect a team leader, team secretary, team editor, and team supply manager. Each group will be known by a color such as blue or red. This color name will be used while visiting the museum and gift shop.

Team Leader:

This person is responsible for the productivity of the group. He/she should make sure that all members are aware of project due dates. He/she insures that the group runs smoothly, handling any problems that might arise. In addition, the leader checks that each team member stays on task and completes his or her assignment in a timely fashion.

Team Secretary:

This person fills in the Cooperative Rain Forest Grid (page 138) and keeps it updated. Secretaries help edit written work.

Team Editor:

This person edits written work with the help of the team secretary. Other team members can be enlisted to help edit also.

Museum Options *(cont.)*

Overview *(cont.)*

Team Supply Manager:

This person gathers all materials necessary for the project. The manager orders what is needed from the teacher when their supplies are low. Additionally, he/she is in charge of supervising and helping clean up. These jobs can be rotated, and additional responsibilities may be added as necessary.

Directions for Option One:

This option allows the Rain Forest Museum to be set up by specific rain forest country or geographic location. The actual construction of the rain forest is very similar for each option. The following steps may be used to guide the student teams in the organization and construction of the Rain Forest Museum.

1. Gather resource materials on plants, animals, products, and people indigenous to the specific rain forest chosen.

2. Compile a list of specific animals (birds, mammals, reptiles, insects, and fish), plants, trees, flowers, vines, water sources, people, and products that will be represented in the group's section of the Rain Forest Museum.

3. Using the forms provided (pages 139–142), research the chosen plant, animal, product, and people.

4. Summarize your research into one or two paragraphs. It would be helpful to use a computer for this activity, as you can print out multiple copies. One could be used for the display itself on a note card, and another copy could be included in a museum guide book.

5. Make rain forest decorations.

Museum Options *(cont.)*

Requirements for Option One Stations:

Check off each item as it is completed. This top portion can also be used with Museum Options Two and Three.

_____   Cards with information found in research to put by displayed items

_____   Research for Museum Guide Book

_____   Identification labels for display items

_____   Museum tour guide speech written on note cards

This station should contain the following items. Each of them should be labeled with an identification label and an information card.

_____   Mammal

_____   Bird

_____   Insect

_____   Snake

_____   Butterfly

_____   Bat

_____   Amphibian and/or Reptile

_____   Epiphyte

_____   Palm Tree

_____   Trees (include buttress or stilt roots)

_____   Liana

_____   Flowering Plant

_____   Water Source-—Optional

_____   Tribal People (housing may be included)

_____   Product

Be certain that the display reflects the four layers of the rain forest. Each plant, animal, etc., should be placed in the appropriate layer.

Museum Options *(cont.)*

Presentation for Option One:

❖ Set up a schedule for classes to visit the museum. Plan on each class spending about an hour in the museum and shop. Invite the local community. Call the local newspaper for coverage.

❖ Notify visitors of their scheduled times. Send student-created or sample invitations (page 155).

❖ Students responsible for each station will use their research to prepare and practice short presentations for museum visitors.

❖ Each station is assigned a color to facilitate tours.

❖ Lay a path on the floor of the museum to show visitors where to go. Dim the lights, start the humidifier, and play a tape of rain forest sounds to create atmosphere.

❖ Classes visiting the museum should be divided into the number of stations at the museum. For instance, if the class has 30 students and the museum has five stations, then six students will be in a station at a time. The first set of students entering the museum are sent to the first station (for example: red station), and so on.

❖ When all the visitors are seated at their stations, the tour guides begin their presentations. Flashlights would be helpful in pointing out specific plants and animals. After a predetermined amount of time (about 2–3 minutes), a signal should be given (hand clap, tone, etc.) All visitors stand and move to the next station. Tour guides give their same presentation again. Continue in this manner until each group has visited every station.

❖ Play the six-minute *Vanishing Rain Forest Rap* video (see Resources, page 166). This will allow time for the museum guides to prepare the gift shop (in an adjacent area).

❖ The gift shop should be set up with the same number of tables as stations in the museum. The students at each station will work at the same color table in the shop.

❖ Groups of students visit the tables in the gift shop in the same manner as they did in the museum. Allow about 2–4 minutes at each table, give the same signal as before, and each group moves to the next table.

❖ When each group has visited all the stations, the class may be dismissed.

Museum Options *(cont.)*

Option Two

Organized by the Different Elements of the Rain Forest

Overview

Cooperative groups will be formed and organized by elements of the rain forest, such as Plants, Animals, People, Products, and Problems. These teams can be organized in the same manner as in Option One (see pages 133 and 134).

Directions for Option Two:

Museum Option Two follows the same steps as Museum Option One except that station organization is done by elements of the rain forest.

Requirements and Presentation for Option Two Stations:

Same as Option One (see pages 135–136)

Option Three

Organized into One Combined Rain Forest

Overview

Each student chooses one plant or animal in which to become an expert. Rain Forest plants and animals will be strategically placed around the classroom in their appropriate settings.

Museum Option Three allows for independent rather than team work. Each student researches and constructs at least one plant or animal. The entire class works together on constructing the leaves, vines, trees, etc., necessary to transform the entire room into a tropical rain forest.

Directions for Option Three:

The first two steps are the same as Options One and Two (see page 134). This option can be presented using less time than the other two, depending on the number of presentations given.

Students will use their research to prepare short presentations for museum visitors.

Requirements for Option Three Stations:

See the top portion of page 135.

Presentation of Option Three:

❖ As each class enters, seat them for the viewing of the six-minute *Vanishing Rain Forest Rap* video.

❖ Dim the lights, start the humidifier, and play a tape of rain forest sounds.

❖ Selected students will act as tour guides during each presentation. They will present their research to the entire visiting group.

❖ Flashlights are effective in highlighting specific plants and animals.

❖ Tour guides will describe and show articles for sale in the museum shop. Visitors will then be allowed to make their purchases.

Cooperative Rain Forest Grid

Team Color _____

Team Leader _____

Team Editor _____

Team Secretary _____

Team Supply Manager _____

Team Members	Project (Construction)		Date		Project Research/Writing		Date	
			Start	Finish			Start	Finish

Animal Research

Name_____ Date_____ Animal _____

Physical Characteristics: (How it looks, moves, etc.)

Habitat: (Include which rain forest and layer.)

Food:

Enemies:

Unique Characteristics:

Other Interesting Information:

Plant Research

Name_____ Date_____ Plant_____

Physical Characteristics: (Include color, size, etc.)

Habitat: (Include which rain forest and layer.)

Seed Dispersal: (Include how this is accomplished.)

Predators:

Unique Characteristics: (Does it flower? How often does it have an aroma?)

Other Interesting Information:

Rain Forest People Research

Name_____ Date_____ Tribe _____

Physical Characteristics: (Include color, size, etc.)

Location: (Include which rain forest.)

Food: (Include how it is obtained.)

Shelter:

Tools and Weapons:

Other Interesting Information: (Include ceremonies.)

Rain Forest Product Research

Name_____ Date_____ Product _____

Type of Product: (food, medicine, etc.)

Location: (Include which rain forest.)

How Is This Product Used Today?

Extractive or Destructive?

Other Interesting Information:

Museum Materials and Construction

To preserve rain forest trees, use of recycled materials is encouraged. Start collecting discarded, reusable materials as soon as possible. A hot glue gun will be a useful tool in constructing your classroom rain forest.

Suggested Materials:

lots of newspaper
construction paper
craft paper
Christmas tree stand
large carpet tubes
scrap wood
empty gallon milk containers
fishing line
brown grocery bags
twigs or branches
papier mâché recipe
cheese cloth or netting
fat yarn
silk plants
balloons

twine or string
hot glue gun
instant papier mâché
overhead or opaque projector
chicken wire
refrigerator and appliance boxes
tissue paper
tempera paint
sponges
large and small gift wrap tubes
industrial-sized aluminum cans
heavy duty tape such as duct tape

plastic trash bags
crepe paper
palm fronds
clay
crepe paper streamers
recycled sheets (dyed green)
macramé cord
real plants
potpourri or potting soil
white glue
play dough or clay
rocks
crayons and/or markers
old stockings

Museum Materials and Construction *(cont.)*

Background

- Empty refrigerator cartons could be cut open and painted with green or greenish-brown tempera paint. Sponge painting may be done on the dried surface with various shades of green to give the background a dappled effect.

- Craft or butcher paper could be hung on the walls or from the ceiling. This could be sponge painted in the same manner as above. A few enormous tree trunks can be painted on this background.

Large Trees

(Make only one or two of each type of tree. Although rain forests have a great variety of trees, only a few of each kind are found in the same area.)

- Large carpet tubes, large gift wrap tubes, large print shop paper tubes, or large aluminum cans from the school cafeteria can easily be made into trees by taping two or more together with duct tape.

- Brainstorm ways to support the trees. The following are some suggestions:

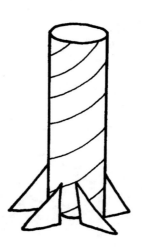

  Use Christmas tree stands.

  Cut four slits at the bottom of each tube. Slide heavy cardboard triangles into the slits. This will simulate buttress roots.

  Scrap wood can be used to make a stand to add support to the trunk.

  Fill empty milk containers with weights such as sand, water, dirt, etc., and tape them around the base of the tree.

  Fill boxes with bricks and rocks and then cut holes in the lids and insert the tree trunk.

  Use heavy duty tape to secure the trunk to the floor.

  Use fishing line from the trunk to the ceiling for support.

- Paint the tubes or cans brown or wrap them with brown craft or crepe paper.

- Crumpled newspaper stuffed inside garbage bags can be wrapped around the trunks to simulate the width of the tree. The bags can be covered with paper or painted to look like bark. This can create various textures. Fringed burlap, jute, or thick yarn can be wrapped around for the vines.

- To create stilt roots use cardboard gift wrap rolls.

- To create strangler fig tree roots use brown crepe paper or twisted kraft paper.

- Add leaves cut from construction paper, tissue paper, or grocery bags painted green. Wire may be added to the leaves so that they can be bent and shaped.

Museum Materials and Construction *(cont.)*

Understory Trees

- Construct understory trees out of tubular fabric bolts, aluminum cans, scrap wood, or twisted craft paper.

- Papier mâché newspaper can be applied to the trunks for width.

- To complete trunks and leaves, follow the same process used for large trees.

- Branches can be made from twisted craft paper, old palm fronds, real twigs and branches, or long cardboard tubes.

- Fruits and nuts can be made from various materials such as clay, papier mâché, construction paper, etc.

Canopy

- Green tissue paper can be used to cover the light fixtures to create a green, shady effect.

- Green crepe paper streamers can be stapled or taped to the ceiling.

- Cheese cloth or netting that has been dyed or painted green can be suspended from the ceiling for a more authentic look.

- Wire can be hung wall to wall, high above the floor. It can be attached to the ceiling with jute for additional support. Recycled sheets can be dyed green, folded in half, and fringed. These can be draped and fastened over the wire.

- Make many different leaves from construction paper, tissue paper, craft paper, crepe paper, grocery bags, etc. Attach to the above to make an umbrella of leaves. Use the patterns provided in this book or have students create their own patterns.

- Vines or lianas can be made from fat yarn, twisted craft or crepe paper, dead grape vines, etc. To use grocery bags, cut out the bottom of the bag. Split the bag in half lengthwise. Spray it lightly with water and then twist it tightly. These can be stapled together to make longer vines. These vines can be looped in and out and through all the layers. Be sure to intertwine them among the trees to give an authentic touch.

- Spanish moss can be attached to the trees.

- Cacao pods, fruit, etc., can be constructed using small balloons covered with several coats of papier mâché. When they are dry, paint and hang them from the trunks and branches of the trees.

- Fruit, such as bananas, can be made from instant papier mâché found in craft stores.

Museum Materials and Construction *(cont.)*

Understory Trees *(cont.)*

Add birds' nests. An interesting bird's nest is the Central American oropendola's, a relative of the oriole. This nest is long and looks like a bag. Nests are found hanging in the trees in groups. To create this nest, inflate a balloon so that it is a teardrop shape. Pull twine, string, or yarn through a 50/50 solution of white glue and water. Wrap layers of the glued twine around the balloon, overlapping to create a woven appearance. The narrow end should have an opening where the bird would enter. Allow the twine to thoroughly dry (it may take a few days), and then pop the balloon. Weave Spanish moss, twigs, or excelsior in and out of the twine to lightly cover the nest. Hang the nest in a tree. (See below.)

Oropendola Bird Nest

Forest Floor

- Many of our house plants originate in the tropical rain forests. Use live or silk plants to decorate the floor of the rain forest.

- Place a container of moist potting soil or rain forest potpourri around the room to add a musty odor.

- Green dyed sheets can be used to cover the floor near the refrigerator cartons.

- To simulate a river or waterfall, use blue cloth samples or blue construction paper covered with blue plastic wrap.

- Cut or tear brown paper bags into leaf shapes and scatter around the floor, or use real leaves.

- A termite mound can be made from a discarded roundish container and painted brown. It could also be constructed from wadding newspaper, wrapping masking tape around it to give it form, covering it with papier mâché, and then painting it. A large balloon can be used as the base. A clever idea is to add fake termites coming and going from the mound.

- A variety of mushrooms can be made from play dough or clay.

- Construction paper can be used to make small shrubs, plants, etc.

Museum Materials and Construction *(cont.)*

Forest Floor *(cont.)*

If space allows, a rain forest hut would make an interesting addition to the rain forest. People of the rain forest have many different types of homes, so the style of the hut can be modified to fit the tribal people represented. Large pieces of cardboard (from an appliance box) can be used for the base of the hut and the roof. Doors and windows should be cut out. The roof should be a conical shape. Use brown craft paper or recycled grocery bags to cover the outside of the hut. Overlap the bags as they are taped to the sides and roof of the hut. Fringe the edges of the bags.

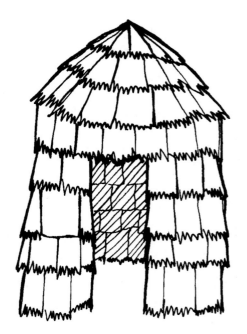

- Appropriate animals should be placed on the rain forest floor.

- If you are fortunate enough to have a fountain supply company nearby, perhaps they will loan you a waterfall.

- Real rocks, moss, leaves, etc., will add a realistic touch.

- Rain forest people can be made in a variety of ways. Have students trace each other onto large pieces of craft paper. Double the paper so two identical forms can be cut out. Paint details on your forms to create "people." Stuff the "people" with newspaper and staple around the edges to seal. Students can make masks of rain forest people. These can be hot glued to the walls of your rain forest, and bodies can be added with paint.

Animals

- Construct a pattern using the overhead or opaque projector.

- To make paper stuffed animals, cut out two identical patterns, paint or color realistic features, staple one side together, stuff with newspapers, finish stapling.

- Papier mâché, chicken wire, old stockings, cardboard tubes, and boxes can be used to form bodies, arms, and legs.

- Recycle materials such as Styrofoam packaging, material scraps, fur scraps, paper plates, pipe cleaners, felt, natural materials (pine cones, Spanish moss, feathers), cans, etc.

- Stuffed animals can be added.

- Students can create animals out of macrame.

Museum Materials and Construction *(cont.)*

Animals *(cont.)*

To make papier mâché animals, demonstrate how to make one animal and then allow the students to construct their own.

Materials:

- lots of newspapers
- masking tape
- cardboard tubes
- aluminum foil
- construction paper
- paper cone

- papier mâché recipe
- balloons (assorted shapes and sizes)
- egg-shaped containers
- wire hangers
- paint

- scissors
- feathers
- assorted materials to add details (jiggle eyes, pipe cleaners, etc.)

1. **Animals:** Form the shape of your animal by crumpling sheets of newspaper into tight wads. Using masking tape, tape the wads together to make a basic form. Heads could be made by wadding up paper or with a small balloon. Tails or legs could be made with wadded paper formed over unbent wire hangers or by bending paper tubes. These should be attached to the body using masking tape. Using your favorite papier mâché recipe, cover the animal with several layers of papier mâché. When the animal form is completely dry, paint the animal to appear realistic.

2. **Birds:** Use an egg-shaped container for the head and an oblong balloon for the body. Cover the egg and oblong balloon with one or two layers of papier mâché strips and allow it to dry. Join the head and body with masking tape and add details—tail (paper tube, bend to shape), wings (folded paper or aluminum foil), beak (paper cone or aluminum foil), legs (wadded paper). Cover the entire form with several layers of papier mâché and allow to thoroughly dry. Paint the bird using resource materials as a guide. Real feathers may be added for authenticity.

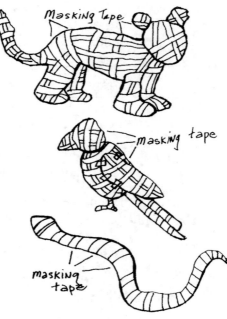

3. **Snakes:** Some rain forest snakes can grow quite large, such as the anaconda (30 feet or 9 meters). Crumple pieces of newspaper into tight wads and tape together with masking tape to form the basic shape of the snake. The snake's body may be coiled or curved. Cover the tightly wadded paper with several layers of papier

Museum Materials and Construction *(cont.)*

Animals *(cont.)*

To make lunch bag animals, provide the following materials and suggestions.

Materials:

- brown lunch bags
- construction paper
- newspaper
- wire
- egg cartons
- grocery bag
- felt
- cotton-tipped swabs
- papier mâché recipe
- hot glue gun

- masking tape
- tempera paint
- pipe cleaners
- white butcher paper
- quilt batting
- yarn
- paper towel tube
- tissue paper
- markers
- paper plates

1. Lunch bags can be stuffed with newspaper and sealed with masking tape.

2. Use masking tape to define neck, body sections, etc.

3. Additional stuffed bags can be connected with masking tape to add legs, tails, etc.

4. Newspaper wads or egg carton sections can be taped on for features such as ears, nose, eyes, feet, arms, etc.

5. Birds' beaks can be made from tagboard, paper plates, or formed from wadded up newspapers.

6. Wire can be inserted into limbs and tails in order to bend them into shape.

7. Long-bodied animals such as snakes and lizards can be formed around paper towel tubes. Twisted newspaper can be inserted into each end of the tube for the head and tail.

8. Spikes and horns can be made from wadding small pieces of newspaper and taping them to the body. Use several layers of papier mâché to cover animal. Allow layers to dry thoroughly.

To add details:

1. Paint animals with realistic colors/features either before or after details have been added, depending on the animal.

2. Real or paper feathers can be added to birds.

3. Pipe cleaners can be used for feet.

4. Felt can be used for eyes or ears.

5. Batting can be glued on to simulate softness, fluffiness, or fur, such as the face of the ring-tailed lemur or aye-aye.

6. Pipe cleaners, wire, or twist ties can be used for claws.

7. Torn tissue or construction paper can simulate scales.

Museum Materials and Construction *(cont.)*

Rain Forest Atmosphere

- Dim the lights and play tapes of rain forest sounds to add atmosphere during museum tours.

- Humidifiers will add a steamy effect.

- Use flashlights to spotlight specific plants and animals during tours.

Rain Forest Mural

- Paint a mural of a tropical rain forest.

- Add trees, plants, animals, etc.

- Sponge painting contributes an exciting effect.

- The mural can be hung outside the classroom to create excitement at the museum entrance and also as an advertisement for the museum.

Museum Gift Shop and Fund-raising Ideas

Now that the students' consciousness has been raised about the plight of the rain forest, it is time to take action. Fund-raising activities, such as a rain forest museum gift shop, can be used to raise money to purchase land for the preservation of tropical rain forests (see Resources, pages 164–167).

The following is a list of successful items that could be successfully sold in your museum gift shop. Allow sufficient time to order and make these items.

- Use companies provided in the Resources section to order rain forest related items to sell. For example: rain forest pencils, animals, safari hats, snakes, fans, etc.

- A rain forest coloring book can be made by having each student design a page.

- Have a T-shirt design contest to create a "Save the Rain Forest" logo. Contact a local T-shirt printing company to reproduce the winning design onto shirts.

- Use rain forest stamps to create stationery. Wrap ribbon around the sheets to make small bundles.

- Use rain forest rubber stamps to create note cards. Wrap ribbon around the sheets to make small bundles.

- Design a clever note pad. Ask a local printer to donate the paper and printing of the note pad.

- Ask local merchants for donated items for the gift shop.

- Purchase plain plastic visors or painters' hats from a supplier like Oriental Trading Company (see Resources). Have students paint rain forest designs and slogans on them.

- Design, color, and laminate book marks.

- Print a recipe book by compiling favorite chocolate recipes.

- Make rain forest chocolate candies using molds.

- Make original chocolate treats. (See Heavenly Chocolate section, pages 100–103.)

- Create rain forest slogan buttons.

- Sell manufactured rain forest theme snacks (see Resources).

Print a price list of items for sale at the Museum Gift Shop and distribute these with class invitations to expedite sales on the day of their visit.

Museum Gift Shop and Fund-raising Ideas *(cont.)*

Additional Fund-raising Ideas

- Hold a bake sale of treats made from products grown in the rain forest.

- Hold a rain forest raffle. Ask for donations from parents or local merchants to include in the raffle. Here are some suggestions for prizes:

spice rack with tropical spices	bath collection with tropical scents
fruit basket with tropical fruits and nuts	trip to the Rain Forest Museum

- "Read for the Rain Forest": Family members and friends pledge to make a weekly contribution when the student reads for a predetermined number of minutes per week.

- Conduct a penny drive. Collect spare pennies to save the rain forest.

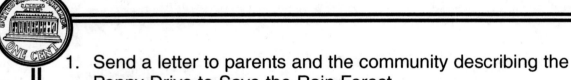

1. Send a letter to parents and the community describing the Penny Drive to Save the Rain Forest.

2. Write a press release to send to local newspapers, radio, and local TV stations describing your activities and asking community people to contribute their pennies.

3. Invite a local celebrity or politician to your school to kick off the campaign.

4. Set up a collection time and place at school for people to drop off pennies.

5. Designate a "Penny Day" to wrap and count the pennies. They could be counted daily or weekly. Invite volunteers to help.

6. Display a large chart illustrating the number of pennies collected.

7. Chart the progress of the Penny Drive to determine the number of acres you will be able to save.

8. Contact a local bank to see if they will send an armored car to pick up the pennies. Ask the bank president to present a check at a special assembly. Invite the press.

Museum and Gift Shop Grand Opening

The students of room _____ are proud to announce the opening of their Rain Forest Museum and Gift Shop. Our museum will contain information about rain forests throughout the world by displaying the vast diversity of life found there. Students will explain the importance of the rain forests and how their loss would affect the world in which we live.

Each class is welcome to visit our Rain Forest Museum and Gift Shop. A price list is attached so that you can help your child pre-select items to purchase. All proceeds from the Gift Shop will be used to buy land for the preservation of tropical rain forests. We hope you will help us with this worthy cause.

Thank you for your cooperation.

_____ class will be visiting the Rain
          (Teacher's name)

Forest Museum on _____
               (Date)

at _____   _____
   (Time)   (Student's name)

All parents and members of the community are invited to visit our Rain Forest Museum and Gift Shop anytime it is open. Our hours will be:

_____

_____

Rain Forest Museum Poster *(cont.)*

Directions: Reproduce and display this sign in the gift shop.

ALL PROCEEDS WILL BE USED TO BUY LAND FOR PRESERVATION OF THE TROPICAL RAIN FORESTS.

Museum and Gift Shop Invitation

Cut along the dashed lines. Fold the invitation along the horizontal line so that pages 2 and 3 are behind pages 1 and 4. Fold along the vertical line that separates pages 1 and 4.

Rain Forest Quiz

Test your knowledge of rain forest facts by using the cards provided.

Directions:

1. Reproduce the numbered questions on the following pages onto tagboard. Cut out into individual question cards. Alternatively, the questions could be duplicated, cut out, and glued onto index cards.

2. Cards can be used by two or three students as a game. Place cards face down in a pile. Players take turns choosing a card to answer. Answers are then checked against the answer key.

3. The teacher could use the cards for various academic games.

4. Additional question cards can be added to this activity.

5. Place cards in an envelope or decorated container for museum visitors. Each visitor can choose one card to answer. Their responses would then be checked against the answer key. A coupon for the museum store could be a reward for a correct response.

Answer Key

1. understory
2. True
3. A: more than 100
4. biodiversity
5. turtle
6. Central & South America
7. B: Borneo and D: Sumatra
8. tusks
9. conservation
10. B: Lepidoptera
11. No
12. metamorphosis
13. bromeliads
14. forest floor, understory, canopy, emergent layer
15. False

16. canopy
17. emergent
18. epiphyte
19. False
20. deforestation
21. D: all of the above
22. C: apple
23. cacao
24. True
25. D: all of the above
26. equator
27. Azteca ant
28. Chico Mendes
29. Slash and burn, cutting trees for lumber, clearing land for cattle, housing, or farming
30. True

Rain Forest Quiz *(cont.)*

1. The _____ is a layer of trees and plants that grows below the canopy.

2. True/False

   One half of the world's species lives in the rain forests.

3. How many different kinds of bats can be found in Costa Rica?

   A. More than 100
   B. more than 1,000
   C. less than 100
   D. none

4. The differences that exist among all living things is called

   _____ .

5. The matamata is the strangest

   _____ in the world.

6. On which continents are the fer-de-lance snake and the emerald tree boa found?

   _____

   _____

7. Orangutans are found on which two islands in Southeast Asia?

   A. Singapore
   B. Borneo
   C. Bali
   D. Sumatra

8. An elephant's two very large teeth are called

   _____ .

9. Using our Earth's natural resources with care is called

   _____ .

10. The scientific name for moths and butterflies is...

    A. butterflies
    B. lepidoptera
    C. arachnids
    D. archaeology

Rain Forest Quiz *(cont.)*

11. Is the expression "blind as a bat" a true statement? _____	12. Frogs and butterflies go through physical changes called _____ .
13. Plants with stiff, spiky leaves that collect rainwater in their cup-like centers are called _____ .	14. The four layers of the rain forest are _____ _____
15. True/False The forest floor is full of sunlight. _____	16. Most plants and animals of the rain forest live in the _____ layer.
17. The tallest layer of the rain forest is the _____ .	18. A plant that grows on another plant but does not harm it is called an _____ . Orchids, ferns and bromeliads are examples of these.
19. True/False Leafcutter ants eat leaves. _____	20. What is possibly the main reason for global warming? _____

Rain Forest Quiz *(cont.)*

21. Rain forest trees and plants are pollinated in which of the following ways...
    A. bats
    B. wind
    C. birds
    D. all of the above

22. Which of the following items do not come from the rain forest?
    A. lemon
    B. banana
    C. apple
    D. chocolate

23. What type of beans produce chocolate?

    _____

24. True/False

    Natural rubber comes from latex.

    _____

25. Rain forests are important because they provide...
    A. oxygen
    B. medicine
    C. rubber
    D. all of the above

26. All of the tropical rain forests are found close to which imaginary line?

    _____

27. Which insect protects the cecropia tree?

    _____

28. Which famous Brazilian rubber-tapper gave his life trying to preserve the rain forest?

    _____

29. What are two causes of rain forest destruction?

    _____

    _____

30. True/False

    A pineapple is a bromeliad.

    _____

Save the Rain Forest

Tropical rain forests exist all over the world in areas that hug the equator. Just for fun, learn how to say "Save the Rain Forest" in other languages.

French	Sauver les Pluie Foret
Italian	Tranne le Pioggia Foresta
German	Sparen das Regen Wald
Spanish	Salvo la Lluvia Monte
Malay	Tolon dia Oujan Utan
Cantonese	Cowmenglokeyee
Touchu	Zumalukh

RAIN FOREST PLEDGE

I promise to help save the world's rain forests.
I will use products that help support the rain forests.
I will encourage others to help save the rain forests.

I will respect nature.
I will conserve energy.
I will be a recycler.
I can make a difference!

_____
(Signature)

_____
(Date)

Rain Forest Leaf Patterns

Banana leaves can grow to an enormous size. Rubber tree leaves are also large, although not as large as banana leaves. Cecropia leaves are relatively small and grow on umbrella-shaped trees. Use the patterns provided with an opaque projector to enlarge onto green paper.

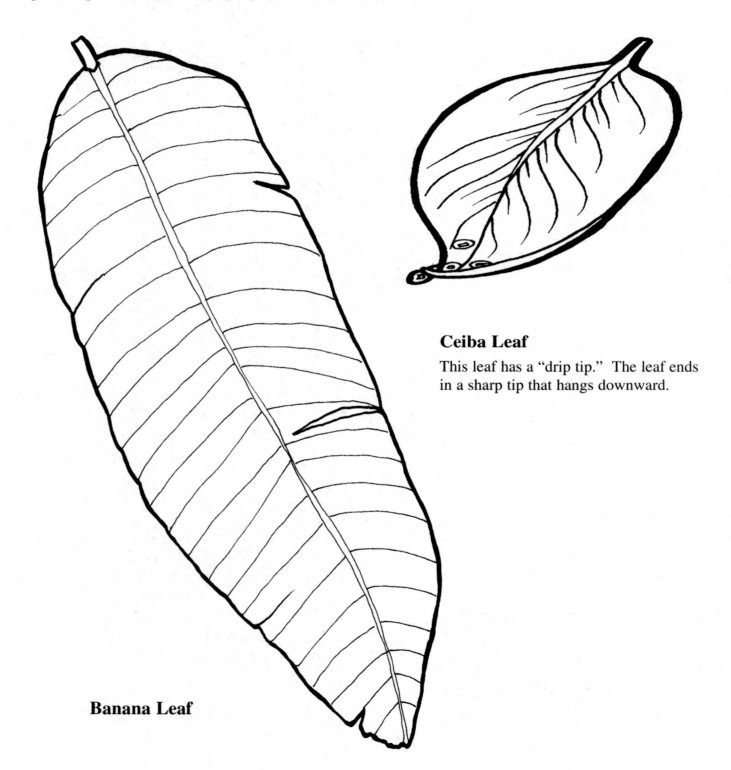

Ceiba Leaf

This leaf has a "drip tip." The leaf ends in a sharp tip that hangs downward.

Banana Leaf

Rain Forest Leaf Patterns *(cont.)*

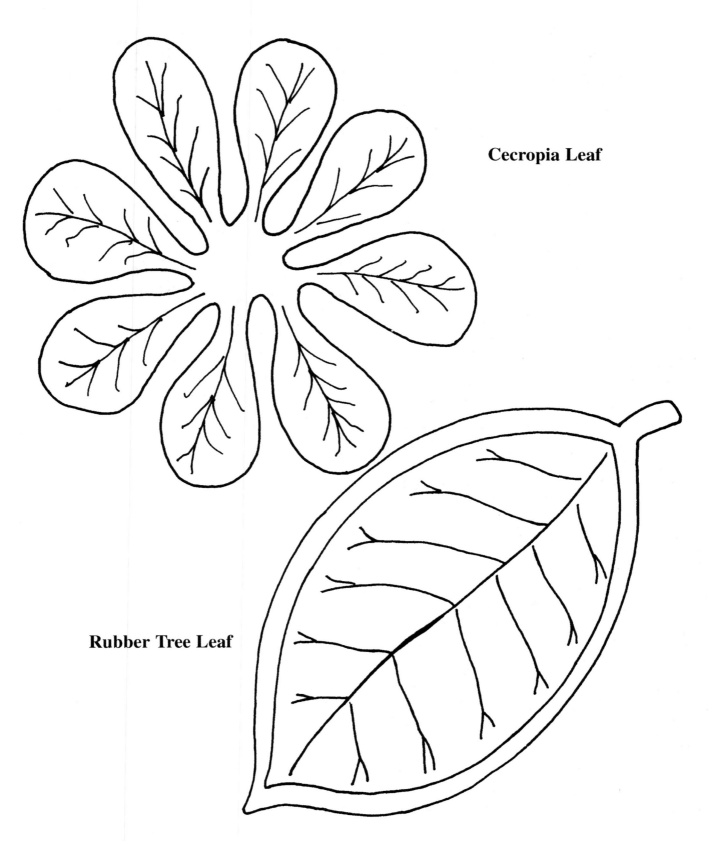

Cecropia Leaf

Rubber Tree Leaf

Unit Management

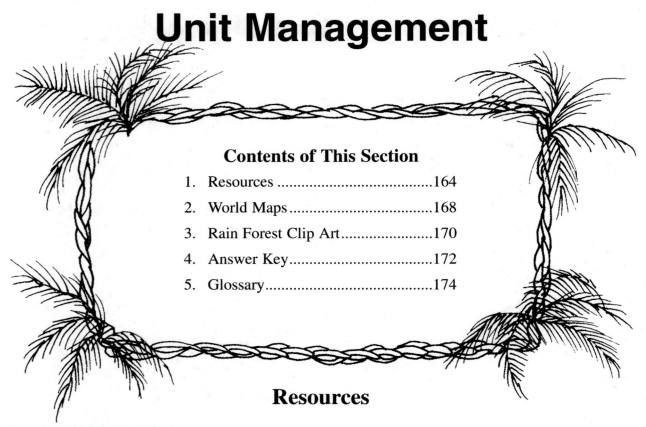

Contents of This Section

Resources

General Reference Books

Ayensu, Edward. *Jungles.* Crown Publishers, 1980.

Caufield, Catherine. *In the Rain Forest.* Alfred A. Knopf Publishers, 1985.

Denslow, Julie Sloane and Christine Padoch. *People of the Tropical Rain Forest.* University of California Press, 1988.

Elkinton, John, Julia Hailes, Douglas Hill, Joe Makower. *Going Green*: *A Kid's Handbook to Saving the Planet.* Penguin Press, 1990.

Javna, John. *50 Simple Things Kids Can Do to Save the Earth.* Andrews and McMeel, 1990. (Contains a variety of environmental issues, problems, and solutions that children can do to help.)

Myers, Norman. *The Primary Source.* Rain Forest Action Network, California, 94133.

Prosser, Robert. *Disapearing Rain Forests.* Dryad Press Limited, 1987. (Discusses causes and consequences of rain forest destruction.)

Sterling, Tom. *The Amazon.* Time-Life Books, 1975.

Student Books

Althea. *Rain Forest Homes.* Cambridge University Press, 1985. (Primary)

Baker, Jeannie. *Where the Forest Meets the Sky.* Scholastic, Inc., 1989. (Intermediate)

Baker, Lucy. *Life in the Rain Forests.* Scholastic-Tab Publications, 1990. (Intermediate)

Banks, Martin. *Conserving Rain Forests.* Steck-Vaughn, 1989. (All ages)

Catchpole, Clive. *The Living World: Jungles.* E.P. Dutton, 1983.

Cherry, Lynne. *The Great Kapok Tree.* Harcourt Brace Jovanovich, 1990. (Intermediate)

Cobb, Vicki. *This Place Is Wet.* Walker and Company, 1989. (Intermediate)

Resources *(cont.)*

Cowcher, Helen; *Rain Forest*. Farrar, Strauss, and Giroux, 1988. (Rain Forest animals and their endangered habitat, beautiful water color illustrations—ages 5–9)

Craig, Janet. *Wonders of the Rain Forest*. Troll, 1989. (All ages)

Dorros, Arthur. *Rain Forest Secrets*. Scholastic, 1990. (Intermediate)

Forsyth, Adrian. *Journey Through a Tropical Jungle*. Simon and Schuster, 1988. (Intermediate)

Galdone, Paul. *The Monkey and the Crocodile*. Ticknow and Fields, 1969. (Primary and Intermediate)

George, Jean C. *One Day in a Tropical Rain Forest*. Thomas Y. Crowell, 1990. (Intermediate)

Gibson, Barbara. *Explore a Tropical Rain Forest*. National Geographic, 1989. (A pop-up book)

Gould, Gill. *Animals in Danger: Forests of Africa*. Rourke, 1982. (Intermediate)

Hale, Tony. *Rain Forest Destruction*. Alladin Books, 1990. (Intermediate)

Lambert, David. *Our Planet: Forests*. Troll Associates 1990. (An overview of rain forest ecology—ages 5–9)

Norden, Carrol R. *The Jungle*. Wisconsin: Mac Donald Raintree Inc., 1987. (Primary and Intermediate)

O'Neill, Mary. *Nature in Danger*. Troll Associates, 1989.

Podendorf, Illa. *Jungles*. Children's Press, 1982. (Primary and Intermediate)

Pratt, Kristin Joy. *A Walk in the Rain Forest*. Dawn Publications, 1992. (Primary and Intermediate)

Prelutsky, Jack. *Toucans Two and Other Poems*. Macmillan, 1970. (A poetry book)

Seuss, Dr., *The Lorax*. Random House, 1971. (Primary and Intermediate)

Van Allsburg, Chris. *Jumanji*. Houghton Mifflin, 1981. (All ages)

Waldrop, Victor, editor. *Wonders of the Jungle*. National Wildlife Federation, 1986. (Intermediate and Advanced)

Wilkes, Angela. *Jungles*. EDC, 1980. (Primary and Intermediate)

Willow, Diane. *At Home in the Rain Forest*. Charlesburg Publications, 1991. (Intermediate)

Wood, John N. and Kevin Dean, *Nature Hide and Seek*. Jungles: Knopf, 1987. (All ages)

Periodicals

"The Canopy," Rain Forest Alliance, 295 Madison Avenue, Suite 1804, New York, New York, 10017 (Published quarterly, contains background information and current topics and events. Available by subscription.)

"The Rain Forests," *National Geographic*, Volume 163, Number 1, January 1983 (An 81-page article with pictures.)

"Save the Rain Forest Updates," Save The Rain Forest, Dodgeville High School, 912 West Chapel, Dodgeville, Wisconsin 53533 (A student-teacher organization that publishes updates on the rain forest, available free of charge.)

"The TREP Action Update: A Newsletter for the Tropical Rain Forest Education Program," Laura K. Marsh, San Francisco State University, Department of Psychology, San Francisco, CA, 94122, (415) 661-1497

Instructional Resources

"Amazon Days, Amazon Nights," audio tape, $7.95 from Natural Resources Defense Council, P.O. Box 1400 Church Hill, Maryland, 21690 (All ages)

"EcoAdventures in the Rain Forest," Computer Program, Chariot Software Group, 3659 India Street, Suite 100C, San Diego, CA 92103-9722

Educator's Rain Forest Workshops to Costa Rica, Belize and Peru. Call Francis Gatz 1-800-669-6806

Resources *(cont.)*

Information on Rain Forest Tribes, Cultural Survival, 11 Divinity Avenue, Cambridge, Massachusetts 02138

"Rain Forest Update Information." Send a self–addressed stamped envelope to: Rain Forest Products, The Needham Science Center, 1155 Central Ave, Needham, Massachusetts 02192

"Sounds of a Tropical Rain Forest in America," CD or audio tape, Carolina Biological Supply Company, 2700 York Road, Burlington, North Carolina 27215 (All ages)

"Tropical Jungle," CD or audio tape with sounds of the tropical jungle, The Nature Company, P.O. Box 2310, Berkley, California 94702 (All ages)

"Txai," Nascimento, Milton, CD or audio tape with songs from the Brazilian Rain Forest

Videotapes and Films

3-2-1 Contact—You Can't Grow Home Again, (One-hour Emmy winning VCR tape on Costa Rican Rain Forest), $19.95 plus $4.95 shipping, the Video Project, 5332 College Avenue, Suite 101, Oakland, CA 94618 (Grades 4–8)

Earth First, (59-minute, 16 mm film or video on the Australian Rain Forest and its destruction, 1987), Educational Film and Video Project, 1529 Josephine Street, Berkley, CA 94703, (415) 849-3163 or 849-1649

Emerald Forest, (90-minute video) available at your local video rental.

Fern Gully, (90-minute animated video) available at your local video rental.

Into Darkest Borneo, (72-minute film on the Penan of Southeast Asia and their effort to save their forest, 1988), World Expeditions, c/o Rain Forest Information Center, Box 368, Lismore, Australia 2480

Ka Tei: Voices of the Land, (21-minute film on the effects of cattle ranching on indigenous people of Costa Rica), Documentary on Films, 4917 Hazel Ave., Philadelphia, Pennsylvania 19143-2004

Our Threatened Heritage, (19-minute film on issues and what is being done about rain forest destruction), 1988, National Wildlife Federation, ATTN: International Program, 1412-16th Street NW, Washington, D.C. 20036

Rain Forest, (Video), National Geographic Society, $26.95, to order, call (800) 368-2728 or Vestron Video, P.O. Box 4000, Stamford, Connecticut 06907

Vanishing Rain Forest Rap, (6-minute video set to rap music with poster and teacher's guide), $36.95, World Wildlife Fund, P.O. Box 4866, Hampden Post Office, Baltimore, Maryland 21211 (Grades 2–6)

Wildlife in the Jungles of Latin America, (Film), International Film Bureau, 332 South Michigan Ave, Chicago, Illinois 60604

Software

"A Day in the Rain Forest," Sunburst Publishers

"Amazon Trail," MECC Software

"Destination: Rain Forest," Imagination Express Series. (an interactive electronics book from Imagination Express).

"Jungle Safari," Orange Cherry Software

"The Rain Forest Volume 4," REMedia Software

Resources *(cont.)*

Laserdiscs

"Biomes: Tropical Rain Forests," Coronet Videodiscs

"Tropical Rain Forests," Modern Curriculum

Miscellaneous

"Wild Places: Monkey Rain Forest," Coronet Videodiscs

"Exploring Rain Forests" program, Steck-Vaughn Support Organizations

Conservation International, 1015 18th Street, NW, Suite 1000, Washington, D.C. 20036

Rain Forest Action Network, 450 Sansome St., Suite 700, San Francisco, California, 94111 (415-398-4404)

The ACEER Foundation, 10 Environs Park, Helena, Alabama 35080 (800) 225-8206

The Nature Conservancy, International Program, 1785 Massachusetts Avenue, NW, Washington, D.C. 20036

The Nature Conservancy/Latin American Division, 1815 North Lynn, Arlington, Virginia 22209, (800) 628-6860

Tropical Ecosystem Research and Rescue, P.O. Box 18391, Washington, D.C. 20036

World Wildlife Fund, 1250 24th Street, NW, Washington, D.C. 20037

People to Write Letters to:

Mr. President, The White House, 1600 Pennsylvania Avenue, NW, Washington, D.C. 20520

Secretary of State, U.S. State Department, 2201 C Street NW, Washington, D.C. 20520

Secretary of Agriculture, U.S. Department of Agriculture, 14th Street & Independence, SW, Washington, D.C. 20250

President, The World Bank, 1818 H Street, NW, Washington, D.C. 20433

Administrator, U.S. Agency for International Development, 320, 21st Street, NW, Washington, D.C. 20577

President, Inter-American Development Bank, 1808 17th Street, NW, Washington, D.C. 20577

Where to Purchase Rain Forest Acreage

Kids for Saving the Earth, P.O. Box 47247, Plymouth, Minnesota 55447-0247

The ACEER Foundation, 10 Environs Park, Helena, Alabama 35080, (800) 255-8206

The Children's Rain Forest, P.O. Box 936, Lewiston, Maine 04240, (207) 784-1069

The Earth's Birthday Project, 170 Joralemon Street, Brooklyn, New York 11201, (718) 834-0516

Supplies for Museum Gift Shop

K&M International, Inc., 1955 Midway Drive, Twinsburg, Ohio 44087, (800) 800-9678

Oriental Trading Company, P.O. Box, 3407, Omaha, Nebraska 68103, (800) 228-2269

Rain Forest Crunch, Community Products, Inc., RD 2, Box 1950, Montpelier, Vermont 05602, (800) 927-2695

Wildlife Artists, Incorporated, 84 North Salem Road, Ridgefield, Connecticut 06877, (800) 444-6945

World Map

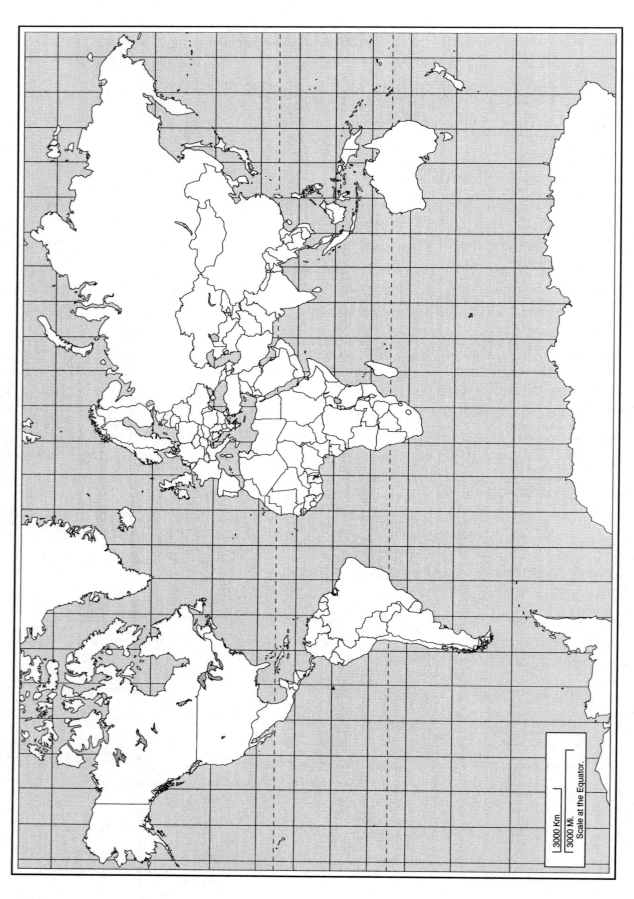

3000 Km
3000 Mi.
Scale at the Equator.

World Map with Rain Forests

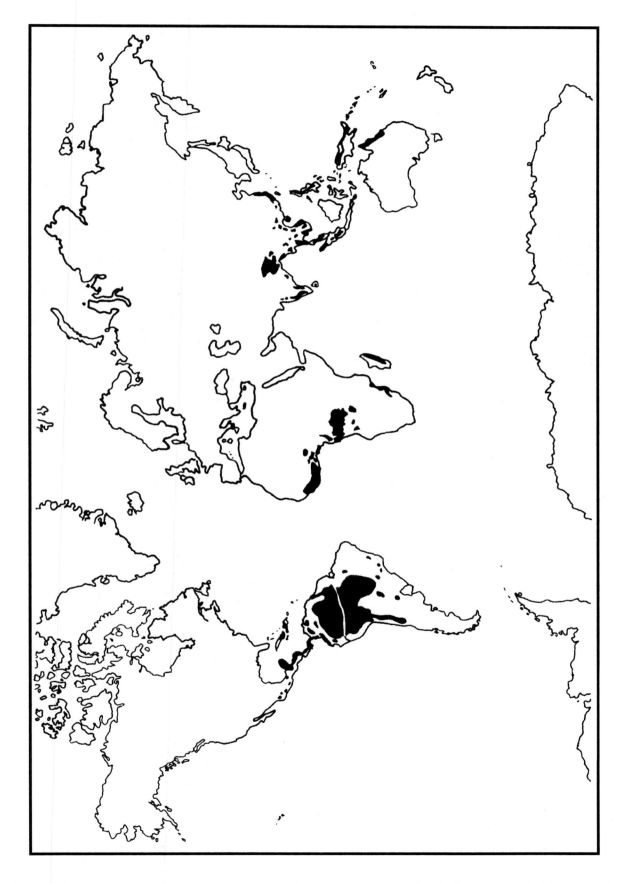

Rain Forest Clip Art

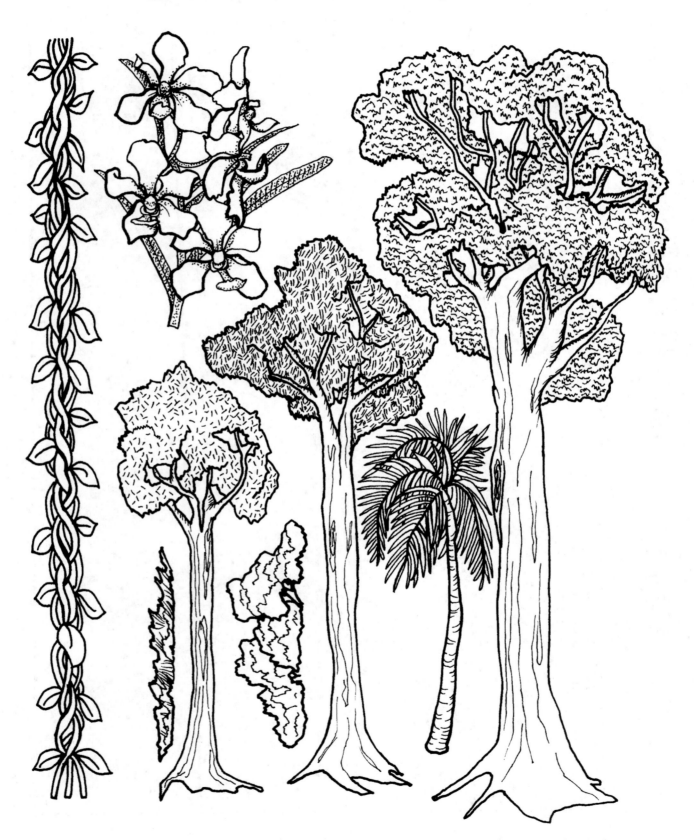

Rain Forest Clip Art *(cont.)*

Answer Key

Tropical Rain Forests of the World...Where Are You?, page 6

1. Tropic of Cancer, Tropic of Capricorn
2. North
3. South
4. Atlantic Ocean
5. North America, Europe, Antartica
6. No
7. Africa
8. False
9. True
10. True

Walk on the Wild Side, page 16

1. V
2. V
3. I
4. I
5. V
6. I
7. V
8. V
9. I
10. V

Going, Going, Gone?, page 29

Birds—Indigo Macaw, Harpy Eagle, Red-Necked Parrot

Reptiles—Radiated Tortoise, African Dwarf Crocodile, Puerto Rican Boa

Amphibians—Panamanian Golden Frog, Monte Verde Toad

Fish—Giant Catfish, Arapaima Fish

Mammals—Aye-Aye, Giant Orangutan, Chimpanzee, Jaguar, Tree Sloth, Howler Monkey, Leopard, Giant Anteater

Canopy Critters, page 48

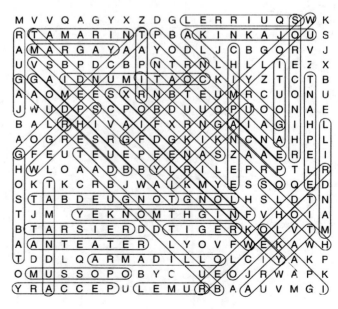

Animal Brain Strain, page 56

Fred: Spider monkey
Harvey: Sloth
Melissa: Tree Frog
Jana: Toucan

Monkeying Around, page 63

1. Bromeliad
2. Monkey
3. Banana
4. Coconut
5. Pineapple
6. Coffee
7. Cinnamon
8. Chocolate
9. Mango
10. Papaya
11. Harpy Eagle
12. Butterfly
13. Sloth
14. Toucan
15. Army Ant
16. Jaguar
17. Macaw
18. Anteater
19. Bat
20. Cobra

Outrageous Orchids, page 69

1. NS
2. S
3. S
4. NS
5. S
6. S
7. S
8. NS

Plant Brain Strain, page 76

David: Fern
Adam: Orchid
Bianca: Kapok Tree
Chelsey: Bromeliad

Answer Key *(cont.)*

Pick a Plant, page 81

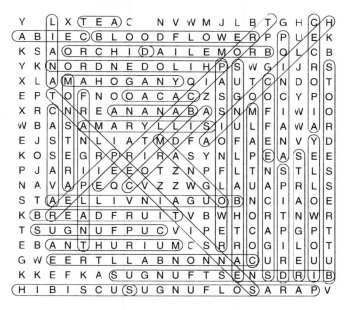

Puzzling Products, page 97

1. coconut
2. papaya
3. vanilla
4. plantain
5. mango
6. yam
7. paprika
8. orchid
9. balsa
10. teak
11. mahogany
12. ginger
13. cucumber
14. cinnamon
15. pineapple
16. eucalyptus
17. quassia
18. cayenne
19. bromeliad
20. patchouli

Chocolate Quiz, page 102

1. cacao beans
2. Hernando Cortez
3. cacao trees
4. Brazil, Central America, the Carribean, Indonesia, West Africa
5. The nib is the innermost part of the cacoa bean and the part that is used in making chocolate.
6. Ivory Coast, West Africa
7. A Greek term meaning seashell
8. a form of currency
9. cacahuatt
10. United States

Chocolate Challenge, page 103

1. Mars
2. Kisses
3. Almond Joy
4. 5th Avenue
5. M & M's
6. Kit Kat
7. Crunch Bar
8. Chunky
9. Clark
10. Baby Ruth
11. Hershey
12. 3 Musketeers
13. Butterfinger
14. Mounds
15. Snickers
16. Milky Way
17. Payday
18. Sugar Babies

People and Products Brain Strain, page 110

Kebe: Cashew Nuts

Alita: Chocolate

Ima: Banana

Alukulu: Mango

Model of Greenhouse Effect, page 123

8. The uncovered jar lost the most heat.
9. It lost less heat because it was covered.
10. Carbon dioxide and water vapor would increase Earth's temperature by preventing heat from escaping into the atmosphere.

Rain Forest Crossword, page 131

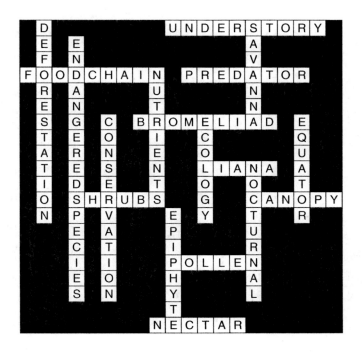

Glossary

adaptation—Changes in the behavior or structure of plants or animals that enable them to survive in their surroundings.

agroforestry—A land-use system in which trees and crops are grown alongside each other. This maintains the forest as a self-renewing resource.

algae—A group of simple plants that usually live in wet and damp places. Many of them are very small.

anthropologist—A person who studies the physical and social characteristics of mankind.

biodiversity—Many different kinds of life in one area.

biome—The largest type of ecological unit, characterized by a distinctive set of plants and animals maintained under the climatic conditions of the region. Examples include deserts and tropical rain forests.

bromeliad—A tropical plant that grows on the branches or trunks of trees. It is a member of the pineapple family.

buttress—A fan-shaped bottom on some of the tall rain forest trees that helps hold the tree upright.

camouflage—The way in which animals avoid the attention of their enemies by resembling or blending in with their surroundings.

canopy—A thick, overhead layer of the rain forest formed by the branches and leaves of the tall trees.

carbon dioxide—A colorless gas that is formed by the combustion and decomposition of organic substances. Carbon dioxide is absorbed from the air by plants in photosynthesis.

cash crops—Agricultural products, such as coffee or bananas, that are sold for profit, often by export, rather than raised for consumption by the producer.

clear cutting—Removing all the trees in a forest, leaving an open patch.

conservation—Protection of natural resources from waste or loss or harm.

decomposer—Organisms, such as bacteria, fungi, and many insects, that break down dead plant and animal materials to be recycled and used by the living.

deforestation—The destruction of a forest. In the tropics, deforestation is caused by a number of activities, such as slash-and-burn agriculture, cattle ranching, and timber harvesting.

development—The alteration of the environment for the benefit of human beings.

diurnal—Refers to animals that are active during the day and rest at night.

drip tips—Leaves that come to a point, allowing rainwater to drip off.

echolocation—The ability of an animal such as a bat or a dolphin to orient itself by the reflection of the sound it produces.

ecology—The study of the environment and the relationship of organisms to it.

ecosystem—A community of animals, plants, and microscopic life that interact in a particular place in the environment.

Glossary *(cont.)*

emergent—The layer of trees in the rain forest that tower in height above others and receive the most sunlight. They can grow to be 200 feet (61 meters) tall.

endangered species—An animal or plant that is threatened with extinction.

environment—All the physical surroundings that are around a person, animal, or plant.

epiphyte—A plant that grows on another plant but does not harm it.

equator—An artificial circle that splits the earth into the northern and southern hemispheres.

erosion—Washing or wearing away of soil.

ethnobotanist—A researcher who studies native plants and their use by the local, indigenous peoples.

exploitation—To use for some purpose for one's own advantage or profit at someone or something else's expense.

extinction—The permanent loss of an animal or plant species.

food chain—The flow of energy (food) among different groups of organisms in a natural community.

forest floor—The bottom layer of the rain forest.

global—A term pertaining to the planet Earth, meaning worldwide or universal.

greenhouse effect—The trapping of heat by the air around the earth.

habitat—An area that provides enough food, water, shelter, and space for an organism to survive and reproduce.

humidity—The amount of water vapor in the air.

hunter-gatherers—People who get most or all of the food they need by hunting and by gathering wild plants.

indigenous—Growing or living naturally in a particular region or environment. The term "indigenous people" is used to mean tribal people.

invertebrates—A group of animals that have no backbone.

jungle—A general term which is interchangeable with the term "tropical rain forest."

liana—A woody vine that is rooted in the soil and grows up tree trunks or in open areas.

mammal—Any animal that feeds its babies with milk from the mother's body.

nature reserve—An area set aside to protect wild plants and animals, often rare ones, that are in danger of becoming extinct.

nectar—A sugary fluid secreted by plants to attract pollinators.

nocturnal—Refers to animals that are active at night and rest during the day.

nutrients—Substances such as vitamins and minerals that are necessary for life.

organic—Of plant or animal origin.

oxygen—A gas that is given off by plants and used by animals.

Glossary *(cont.)*

ozone layer—The region of concentrated ozone that shields the earth from excessive ultraviolet radiation.

parasite—An organism dependent upon another living organism for support or existence.

photosynthesis—A process in which plants convert carbon dioxide into water and sugar.

pollen—Powder-like microspores produced by the flower, containing the male sex cell.

pollination—The transfer of pollen from the male reproductive organs to the female in seed plants.

predator—An animal that hunts or traps other animals for food.

prey—An animal that is caught and eaten by a predator.

rain forest—A very dense forest in a region, usually tropical, where rain is very heavy throughout the year.

reforestation—The action of renewing forest cover by planting seeds or young trees.

resource—A product of the environment which has use or value.

seed dispersal—The way that seeds travel from the parent plant to the ground by wind, gravity, or animals.

slash-and-burn agriculture—The method of agriculture in which people clear land by cutting down patches of forest and burn the debris.

soil erosion—The washing away of soil by wind and water due to the lack of protection of the thin layer of top soil.

species—A group of organisms that have the same traits and can produce offspring that can also produce offspring.

sustainable development—Development that uses natural resources in an efficient way and without destroying the basis of their productivity. It allows natural resources to regenerate.

threatened species—Any species of indigenous plant or animal that could become endangered in the near future if the factors causing its population decline are not reversed.

topsoil—The surface soil, including the organic layer where plants have most of their roots.

tropical—Hot, humid zone between the Tropic of Cancer and the Tropic of Capricorn.

tropical rain forest—An evergreen forest located at low elevations in regions between the Tropic of Cancer and the Tropic of Capricorn. Tropical rain forests are characterized by abundant rainfall and a very warm, humid climate year round.

understory—The layer growing under the canopy. This layer is comprised of shrubs, herbs, and young trees.

vertebrates—The group of animals which have internal skeletons with backbones.